RESEARCH REPORT  MAY 2014

# Preschool Attendance in Chicago Public Schools

Relationships with Learning Outcomes and Reasons for Absences

Stacy B. Ehrlich, Julia A. Gwynne, Amber Stitziel Pareja, and Elaine M. Allensworth
with Paul Moore, Sanja Jagesic, and Elizabeth Sorice

# TABLE OF CONTENTS

**1** Executive Summary

**5** Introduction

### Chapter 1
**9** The Extent of Absenteeism in Preschool and the Early Grades

### Chapter 2
**17** Preschool Attendance and Primary Grade Outcomes

### Chapter 3
**25** Reasons for Preschool Absences

### Chapter 4
**37** Interpretive Summary

**41** References

**43** Appendices

**57** Endnotes

---

**ACKNOWLEDGEMENTS** We would like to acknowledge the many people who contributed to this work through their partnership, support, encouragement, and feedback. This work is the result of a collaboration between the University of Chicago Consortium on Chicago School Research (UChicago CCSR) and the Office of Early Childhood Education at Chicago Public Schools (CPS), with funding from the McCormick Foundation. From CPS, Serah Fatani, Noriko Magari, and Sheila O'Connell were critical partners throughout every stage of the project. They not only provided us with essential data for this research, but they also supported our efforts in data collection, gave feedback on research questions and findings, and collaborated on dissemination activities. Elizabeth Mascitti-Miller has already started to incorporate the implications of key findings from this study into preschool programs across the district. We also thank Barbara Bowman for having the foresight and conviction to learn more about how absenteeism affects preschool children in the district, which was the impetus for this research.

Our collaboration with The McCormick Foundation was equally important. This project was generously funded by the McCormick Foundation, and Sara Slaughter, Lindsay Alvis Cochrane, and Erika Okezie-Phillips at the Foundation were important thought partners at every phase of this work. They provided critical feedback on research questions and findings, but most important, they pushed us to think carefully about how to make this work relevant and meaningful for schools, teachers, and preschool students and their families.

The authors also benefited from the feedback and support from our colleagues at UChicago CCSR. We want to thank Stuart Luppescu for his work analyzing the Kindergarten Readiness Tool (KRT) data; Laney Shaler, Eric Brown, Michelle Huynh, and Josie Glore for assistance with data collection, transcription, and analysis; Lauren Sartain and Eliza Moeller for their detailed comments on draft versions of this work; and Jennifer Cowhy, Holly Hart, and Valerie Michelman for their careful technical read. Emily Krone provided countless hours of support and feedback, always finding ways to improve our writing and message.

We are also grateful for the opportunity to connect this work with that of Hedy Chang of Attendance Works. Hedy works tirelessly to connect the research focusing on attendance and with practitioners in the field nationwide.

As always, we are indebted to the members of our Steering Committee, who exhibited engagement and excitement over this work. A special thank you goes to Kim Zalent and Reyna Hernandez for their careful read of this document and their feedback.

---

This report was produced by UChicago CCSR's publications and communications staff: Emily Krone, Director for Outreach and Communication; Bronwyn McDaniel, Communications and Research Manager; and Jessica Puller, Communications Specialist.

Graphic Design: Jeff Hall Design
Photography: Cynthia Howe
Editing: Ann Lindner

05.2014/pdf/jh.design@rcn.com

PRESCHOOL ATTENDANCE IN CHICAGO PUBLIC SCHOOLS

# Executive Summary

Significant attention is currently focused on ensuring that children are enrolled in preschool. However, regular attendance is also critically important. Children with better preschool attendance have higher kindergarten readiness scores; this is especially true for students entering with low skills. Unfortunately, many preschool-aged children are chronically absent. They often miss preschool for health reasons, but many families also face a range of logistical obstacles in getting their children to preschool every day.

Consistent school attendance is a foundation of student learning. While missing one or two days of school each year is not likely to have serious consequences, chronic absenteeism is related to significantly lower outcomes for students. Research shows that chronic absenteeism undermines the academic performance of adolescents.[1] And new research suggests that absenteeism is not only a problem among adolescents but also is a significant problem among very young students: 11 percent of kindergarteners across the nation are chronically absent. Kindergarten students who miss more school learn less during the school year.[2] While policymakers and others might be tempted to assume that attendance similarly affects students in kindergarten and preschool, there is very little research on attendance in the preschool years and whether it matters for learning outcomes. Given that many children start their formal schooling in preschool and because the promise of preschool is to prepare children for kindergarten, it is critical to know whether absenteeism undermines that promise.

To address this gap in research, the University of Chicago Consortium on Chicago School Research (UChicago CCSR) partnered with the Office of Early Childhood Education at the Chicago Public Schools (CPS) in 2011 to study absenteeism among CPS preschool students. This report outlines key findings from this study. It describes the extent of absenteeism among preschool students and compares it with absenteeism among students in kindergarten through third grade; examines the relationship between preschool absenteeism and learning outcomes, both during preschool and in second grade; and explores reasons why preschool students miss school.

## Summary of Key Findings

Preschool students miss a lot of school.

- In 2011-12, 45 percent of three-year-old preschool students and 36 percent of four-year-old preschool students were chronically absent—meaning they missed at least 10 percent of their enrolled days, or a minimum of 15 days, over the course of a full school year.

- Regular attendance improves substantially between preschool and kindergarten. In 2011-12, the percentage of kindergarten students who were chronically absent was 20 percent, half the rate of preschool students. This improvement continues into the early elementary grades.

- Some groups of students are much more likely to be chronically absent than others. Racial differences are particularly stark: African American students are almost twice as likely as white, Latino, and Asian students to be chronically absent. Chronic absenteeism is also higher among students who live in high-poverty neighborhoods than among students who live in moderate- or low-poverty neighborhoods. Even after taking into account neighborhood poverty, however, African American preschool students are still much more likely to be chronically absent than other students who live in neighborhoods with similar levels of poverty.

**Students who miss more preschool end the year with lower skills; this relationship is strongest for students with low incoming skills.**

- The more days of preschool a student misses at age four, the lower s/he scores on the math, letter recognition, and social-emotional portions of CPS's Kindergarten Readiness Tool (KRT) at the end of the school year, controlling for entering skills upon entering preschool.
- Students who miss the most preschool are those with the lowest incoming skills.
- Controlling for skills upon entering preschool, good attendance is more strongly related to academic gains for students who enter preschool with lower incoming skills than for students who enter with higher incoming skills.

**Students who are chronically absent in preschool are five times more likely to be chronically absent in second grade. Students who are chronically absent for multiple years between preschool and second grade are in need of intervention to read at grade level by third grade, on average.**

- Preschool attendance is related to chronic absenteeism in kindergarten, a detrimental pattern that often continues into elementary school. While just 7 percent of non-chronically absent four-year-old students go on to be chronically absent in kindergarten, roughly one-third of chronically absent four-year-old preschoolers continue to be chronically absent kindergarteners.
- The relationship between preschool attendance and attendance in later years continues into the elementary grades: chronically absent preschool children are five times more likely to be chronically absent in second grade than their non-chronically absent preschool peers.
- Students who are chronically absent between preschool and second grade have significantly lower learning outcomes at the end of second grade than their counterparts who are not chronically absent in the early years.
- Each successive year of chronic absenteeism compounds the risk. In fact, second-graders who have been chronically absent every year since preschool are, on average, close to the threshold for needing intensive reading intervention in order to be reading at grade level by third grade.

**For all students, health is the most commonly reported reason children miss preschool; a variety of logistical obstacles are secondary.**

- More than half of all the days missed in preschool were due to children being sick, according to attendance logs recorded over a nine-week period.
- Another 18 percent of days missed were due to a range of reported logistical obstacles for families, including difficulties getting children to and from school, child care issues, and multiple family-related matters.
- Many of these logistical obstacles arise because of difficulty with half-day preschool schedules, according to interviews with parents. Half-day programs require that parents find child care for the remainder of the day and arrange drop-off/pick-up in the middle of the day.

**African American and Latino students are sick more often than white students, and African American families report facing many more logistical obstacles.**

- Nearly all preschool students were likely to be sick over the school year, but African American and Latino students missed almost twice as many days due to sickness than white students, according to attendance log data.
- African American students are also much more likely than white or Latino students to face a logistical obstacle in getting to school. Not only were there higher proportions of African American students missing school because of logistical challenges, but those who did encounter these struggles each missed more days of school than white or Latino students who encountered similar struggles.

**Particular family circumstances are related to higher absences for children. The gap in attendance across racial/ethnic groups is partially explained by differences in these family circumstances.**

- Children who faced the following family circumstances had higher preschool absences: being in a single-parent family; having parents with poorer health; using the emergency room for primary medical care; and having a parent who is either unemployed or employed but without a college degree.

- As these circumstances pile up for families, attendance gets worse. Children in families without any of the aforementioned circumstances missed roughly 5.6 percent of school; those with one obstacle missed 7.5 percent; those with two missed 9.0 percent; and those with three or more missed 12.9 percent.

- Many of the family circumstances associated with lower preschool attendance are disproportionately experienced by African American families and, in some cases, Latino families; this contributes to their children's higher absence rates compared to white children.

**Parent beliefs and school culture also may play a role in how often children attend preschool.**

- Parents with stronger beliefs about the importance of regular attendance in preschool also had children with better attendance. In particular, parents who believed that regular attendance in preschool is as important as in later grades had children with the lowest absence rates (7.5 percent); those whose parents said that attendance in preschool is important but would be more important in later years had higher absence rates (10.7 percent); and children whose parents did not believe that regular attendance in preschool mattered much had the highest absence rates (13.2 percent).

- Safe schools, schools in which there is strong parent involvement, and schools in which trust in teachers is strong have better preschool attendance than schools in which these factors are lacking.

## Summary

Both state and federal policies have increasingly focused on early education, aiming to make preschool universally available to three- and four-year-old children. Despite decades of research on the effects of preschool education, the focus has been solely on whether or not enrollment in preschool is beneficial; only recently has attention turned to whether attendance in preschool matters once students are enrolled.

This study suggests that ensuring preschool students attend regularly is a critical component in preparing them for kindergarten and beyond, particularly for students who have low levels of prior skills. Schools may not be able solve all of the issues that keep students from coming to school, but they can work on strategies to get students to school despite those issues. And these strategies can be integrated with other efforts in a school, such an existing Response to Intervention (RtI) model. A critical first step in improving preschool students' attendance is collecting attendance data and monitoring it at the student and school levels. Monthly or biweekly watch lists that highlight those students who miss more than a particular number of days may prove useful, so that teachers can reach out to parents to help develop strategies for attending more regularly. Sharing preschool attendance records with kindergarten teachers as students transition to the next grade level may help elementary schools maintain a sustained and consistent approach to improving attendance over time.

Developing a strong and trusting relationship between school staff and parents may also play a role in improving students' attendance. As parents become directly involved in their child's learning and have stronger relationships with their child's teacher, there is a greater support for academic advancement and more opportunities for school staff to convey the importance of regular attendance in preschool. More targeted efforts may be necessary for students who enter preschool with low levels of incoming skills. These students are the most likely to miss a large amount of preschool, and they benefit the most from regular attendance. It may help to reach out to these parents and build a partnership at the beginning of the school year, before the student is frequently absent, to develop strategies for students' learning that include regular attendance.

Strong connections between schools and families may also provide an opportunity for school staff to better understand the particular challenges parents face in getting their children to school. Improving attendance of very young children is likely to require a "student by student, family by family" approach. While schools cannot reasonably be expected to solve many of the issues that lead to very high rates of absenteeism (e.g., poor family health, child care, and lack of access to quality medical care), they may be able to partner with community organizations that can assist with some of these challenges or figure out ways to help families to support each other. Community partnerships may prove particularly useful in several areas that substantially contribute to preschool absences (e.g., poor student and family health, and the half-day preschool schedule) and may also utilize parents to reach out to other parents, helping to create social networks for families of young children.

# Introduction

Preschool education has become a priority at both the federal and state level, based in large part on decades of research documenting the long-term benefits of early education. However, much of this research focuses on whether or not simply being enrolled in preschool is beneficial. This study attempts to go further by examining whether students enrolled in preschool attend regularly and the extent to which preschool attendance is related to later outcomes.

Preschool education has come to the forefront of conversations on national education policy. In February 2013, U.S. President Barack Obama proposed making preschool universally available to all four-year-old children. This follows a number of state-level policies, including one in 2006 by the state of Illinois, to make preschool universally available to three- and four-year-old children. Both the state-level efforts and Obama's policy initiative are motivated by research showing that high-quality early education can better prepare children for kindergarten and lead to improved long-term outcomes, particularly for disadvantaged children.[3] Yet, despite decades of research on the effects of preschool education, questions have largely focused on whether or not *enrollment* in preschool is beneficial. What has not been investigated is the extent to which students who enroll in preschool attend regularly, and whether *attendance* in preschool matters once students are enrolled.

Research on older students shows that those with better attendance in school have better learning outcomes; they earn higher grades, fail fewer classes, and are more likely to graduate.[4] For older children, attendance is both a key component of achievement (those who attend more school have more opportunities to learn) and an indicator of whether students are likely to struggle with attendance and/or academics in the future. But the extent to which attendance at the preschool level works in the same way is not known. To address this gap in research, the University of Chicago Consortium on Chicago School Research (UChicago CCSR) partnered with the Office of Early Childhood Education at Chicago Public Schools (CPS) in 2011 to study absenteeism among preschool students in CPS. Our study includes three areas of inquiry. First, we document the scope of absenteeism in preschool and examine which students are most likely to be chronically absent. Second, we examine whether attendance during preschool is related to student outcomes. These include kindergarten readiness by the end of preschool, ongoing attendance patterns through second grade, and reading outcomes at the end of second grade. Lastly, we explore reasons why preschool students miss school. The following sections discuss each of these research questions in more depth.

## What is the Extent of Absenteeism Among Preschool Students?

Currently, there is only limited evidence documenting how often young children are absent from school, but that evidence suggests that absenteeism rates are high: nationally, more than 11 percent of kindergarten students are chronically absent, missing more than 18 days, or three to four weeks per year.[5] Among preschool students, absenteeism may be even higher. A recent study released by the Baltimore Education Research Consortium (BERC) was the first to document how prevalent absenteeism is for preschool students, showing that more than one-third of preschoolers in Baltimore are chronically absent.[6] These rates seem high but, given the dearth of comparative information, it is hard to know whether they are specific to Baltimore or indicative of national trends in preschool absenteeism. The present study adds to the understanding of the scope of preschool absenteeism by investigating what preschool attendance looks like in Chicago. In Chapter 1, we answer the questions: *What are average attendance rates among preschool students in Chicago Public Schools, and how many students are chronically absent during preschool? Among preschool students, who is most likely to be chronically absent?*

## Is Preschool Attendance Tied to Students' Academic Success—Both in Preschool and Beyond?

Although school attendance is related to learning outcomes for older students, there is little evidence that it works in the same way during the preschool years. In fact, there are several reasons to think it might not. For example, while enrollment in high-quality preschool programs increases children's preparedness for kindergarten, research is not clear about the amount of exposure during the school day or week preschool children need to achieve this goal. If only a small amount of exposure is needed, then how regularly a student attends preschool may not matter all that much. This may be particularly true in Chicago, where most programs run for only half of the day (2.5 to 3 hours), and therefore daily absences refer only to missing a short amount of school.

On the other hand, if attendance is indeed associated with learning outcomes in preschool, the relationship may be stronger for students who enter preschool with the weakest academic skills, who may also be the children who benefit most from enrollment in preschool.[7] Low levels of attendance for these children may mean that they have less time in the classroom to develop kindergarten readiness skills—both academic knowledge and social-emotional behaviors—that other students may develop at home. Low attendance may also be an indicator that other aspects of their lives are preventing them from attending school regularly and are hindering their learning in preparation for kindergarten. To address the current lack of evidence around whether preschool attendance matters, Chapter 3 answers the questions: *Is attendance in preschool related to learning outcomes in preschool, including the development of letter recognition, pre-literacy, math, and social-emotional skills? If so, is the relationship between attendance and learning outcomes the same for different groups of students, including those with different socioeconomic backgrounds or different levels of incoming achievement?*

Attendance in preschool may serve another purpose: identifying students who are most likely to struggle with attendance, and also learning, in future years. Can attendance in the early years provide information that identifies which students will be most likely to present these patterns of disengagement when they are older? Preschool may be too early—preschool children are often sick, so attendance during preschool may not be a very good indicator of attendance in later grades. However, if patterns of behavior do begin early on, preschool may be the first opportunity to identify students most likely to exhibit low attendance and low levels of learning in future years. Because we know very little about attendance in preschool and the patterns that persist in the early elementary years, Chapter 2 also presents evidence on the following question for students in Chicago: *To what extent is preschool attendance related to attendance and learning outcomes in later grades?*

## Why are Students Absent from Preschool?

Once we understand how absences are related to learning outcomes, knowing the reasons why preschool students miss school, and whether these reasons differ across groups of students, is critical to addressing the problem. Although we have some understanding of why older children miss school,[8] the specific reasons why preschool children are absent have not been carefully documented. This is a significant deficiency because the preschool context is quite different from the older grades, requiring different strategies for improving attendance. Young children are sick more often than older children and more likely to miss school as a result.[9] Quality of health, even among young children, can differ significantly depending on background characteristics, meaning that some preschool students may be more likely to miss school due to sickness than others, depending on their race/ethnicity or socioeconomic status.[10] For example, children from lower socioeconomic families are more likely to have serious health issues and also more likely to be chronically absent.[11] In addition, young children are much more reliant than older children on their parents and other family members to get to school, so family circumstances may also play a greater role in whether a preschool student has good attendance. In Chapter 3, we explore the following questions: *What are the reasons why preschool students are absent from school? How do these reasons differ for white, Latino, and African American students?* In addition to examining reasons for preschools students' absences, we also ask: *What types of family circumstances and parental beliefs are related to attendance for CPS preschool students?*

While reasons for absences among preschool students may be strongly associated with health and family circumstances, schools may also play a role. Research on elementary students suggests that schools with high levels of safety and order, engaging instruction, teacher professional capacity, and parent involvement are more likely to show improvements in student outcomes, including attendance.[12] Extending this question to preschool students has yet to be explored, and so we examine school-level factors and ask: *Does school context play a role in whether preschool students are frequently absent?*

## Who We Studied

This study focused specifically on three- and four-year-old children served by school-based preschool programs in CPS between 2008-09 and 2011-12.[13] The study did not include children who either were enrolled in Montessori programs or were in self-contained

### Do CPS Preschool Students Attend Their Local, Neighborhood Schools for Preschool or Do They Attend Preschool at Other Sites?

In Chicago, there is a considerable amount of school choice, even at the elementary school level. At the preschool level, an array of options are available both in schools and in community-based settings. Because this research focuses on preschool students in CPS, we describe the options for those families choosing to send their children to CPS programs. Unlike students in kindergarten and beyond, preschool students do not have an assigned "neighborhood" school based on where they live. Instead, parents of preschool aged children are required to submit applications to schools they are considering, and schools make the decisions about who to enroll, based on eligibility requirements put forth by their program funders.[A] Given this context, we found that only 41 percent of preschool students attended a preschool housed in an elementary school that would be their assigned neighborhood school in a later grade (Table 1).[B] This is 26 percentage points lower than that of kindergarten students; more than 66 percent of kindergarteners attend their neighborhood school.[C]

Among four-year-olds transitioning into kindergarten, almost 60 percent chose to stay in the same school they attended for preschool (**see Table 1**).

The other 41 percent of students entered different schools when they transitioned into kindergarten. As discussed later in this report, monitoring attendance in both preschool and kindergarten may be a viable to way to intervene with families that need the most support in getting their child to school regularly. With so many students moving to a different school between preschool and kindergarten, this may be a challenge for the district.

**TABLE 1**

**Fewer preschoolers attend their local school compared with kindergarten students, but 60 percent stay in the same school from preschool into kindergarten.**

| | |
|---|---|
| Percent of preschoolers who attend their "neighborhood" school in preschool | 40.6% |
| Percent of kindergarten students who attend their neighborhood school | 66.4% |
| Percent of preschoolers (four-year-olds) attending the same school the following year when they are in kindergarten | 59.0% |

**Note:** Calculations were based on four-year-old preschool students in the 2010-11 school year and kindergarten students in the 2011-12 school year.

special education programs. In each of the four years we studied, CPS enrolled around 26,000 preschool students in four different school-based programs, including Preschool for All (PFA), Head Start, Child-Parent Centers (CPC), and tuition-based programs. Although we did not study differences between the preschool programs within CPS, it is worth noting that, unlike K-12 education, early childhood programs are funded through a number of different funding streams that each has a different governance.[14] One way in which funding differences affect a program is by determining whether it is a half- or full-day program. During the years of our study, most preschoolers in CPS attended half-day programs—meaning they were in school for two-and-a-half or three hours per day. However, children in tuition-based programs and some children in CPC programs attended full-day programs.

About half as many students attend CPS preschools at age three than at age four, and they tend to have higher risk-factors than four-year-old preschoolers. This is likely due to the funding stipulations of preschool programs; public funding for preschool is prioritized for four-year-olds who will be entering kindergarten the following year. A small portion of funds is dedicated to three-year-olds who have high risk-factors for academic failure. Three-year-olds during the 2011-12 school year were more likely than four-year-olds to be African American (44 vs. 34 percent) and from high-poverty neighborhoods (21 vs. 15 percent of four-year-olds; see Figure 1). Four-year-old preschool students were similar to kindergarten students in terms of overall background characteristics, even though many children enter the CPS system for the first time in kindergarten.[15]

**FIGURE 1**

Within the preschool population, three-year-olds are slightly more disadvantaged than four-year-olds, while four-year-olds are similar to kindergarteners

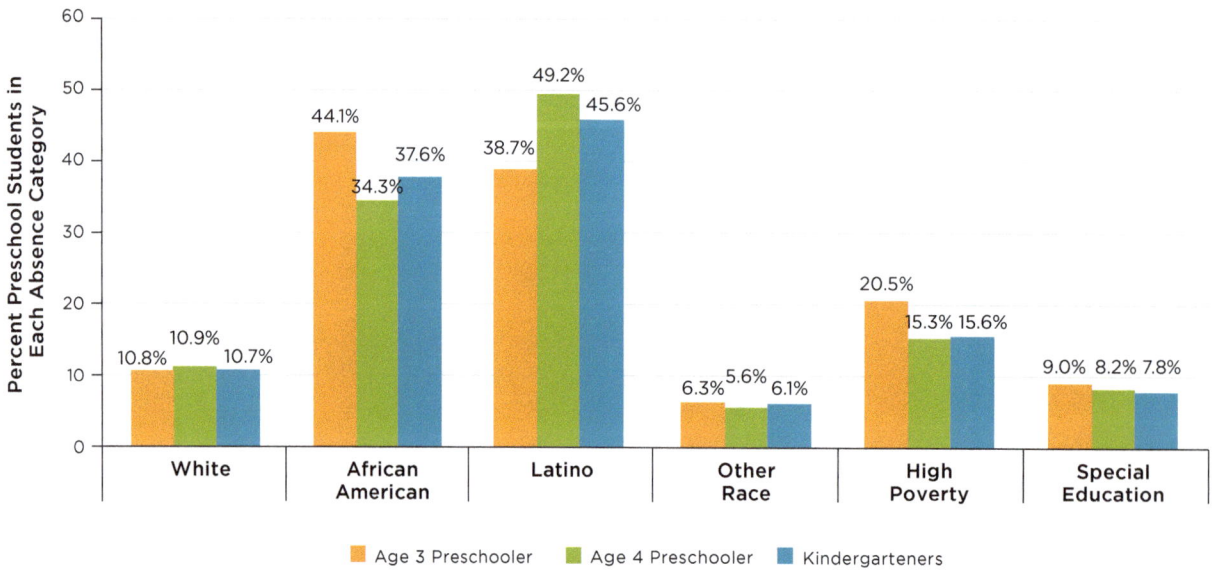

**Note:** Data are based on students who were enrolled in preschool and kindergarten during the 2011-12 school year. The number of students at each age/grade level are: age 3 preschoolers=8,741, age 4 preschoolers=15,971, and kindergarteners=31,010.

CHAPTER 1

# The Extent of Absenteeism in Preschool and the Early Grades

This chapter shows that chronic absenteeism in CPS preschool programs is extremely common: almost half of all three-year-old students and more than one-third of all four-year-old preschoolers are chronically absent. However, students start attending school more regularly as they move into kindergarten and the early elementary school grades. The biggest improvement in attendance occurs between preschool and kindergarten, even though neither preschool nor kindergarten is compulsory in the state of Illinois. Students' race is strongly associated with attendance, more so than neighborhood poverty; African American preschool students are almost twice as likely to be chronically absent as students who are Latino, white, or of another racial/ethnic background. In Chapter 3, we examine the race gaps in attendance and explore some of the reasons African American preschool students miss more school than either white or Latino preschool students.

## How Prevalent is Absenteeism in Preschool?

Preschool students have very high absence rates, but attendance improves as students enter the early elementary grades.

Although there have been improvements in preschool attendance in CPS over the last few years, three- and four-year-old preschool students still miss a lot of school. In 2011-12, three-year-old preschoolers missed an average of 12.5 percent of the school year, and four-year-olds missed almost 10.5 percent (see Figure 2). This means the typical preschool student in CPS was chronically absent, missing at least 10 percent of school.

When students enter kindergarten, their absence rates improve substantially. Over the four years we studied, absence rates for five-year-olds were at least four percentage points better than for three- and four-year-olds. Attendance continued to improve incrementally as students moved through early elementary school. For third-graders, average absence rates were around 5 percent.

Another way of describing absenteeism is by looking at how many students were chronically absent at each age. In 2011-12, 45 percent of three-year-olds and 36 percent of four-year-olds in CPS were chronically absent (see Figure 3). Of these students, at least one-third missed 20 percent or more of school. Over the full school year, this is equivalent to missing 30 days, or at least six weeks (see Defining "Attendance" on p.11). Chronic absenteeism declines as students get older—20 percent of five-year-olds were chronically absent, and this decreased to 10 percent of eight-year-olds.

## Who is Most Likely to be Chronically Absent?

African American preschool students are more likely to be chronically absent than other students.

Chronic absenteeism is more prevalent among some groups of preschool students than others. In particular, African American students are much more likely to be chronically absent than students of any other racial or ethnic group. And students from high-poverty neighborhoods are more likely to be chronically absent than students who live in low- or moderate-poverty neighborhoods (see Appendix A, p.43 for our definitions of neighborhood poverty). Because race and neighborhood poverty are linked, with African Americans more likely to live in high-poverty neighborhoods, we looked at the relationship of each with chronic absenteeism, while taking the other into account. We found race has a stronger relationship with chronic absenteeism, even after we consider student's neighborhood poverty level. African American preschool students from low- or moderate-poverty neighborhoods are about twice as likely to be chronically absent as white students from similar neighborhoods, and over 1.5 times more likely to be chronically absent as Latino students or students of other races/ethnicities from neighborhoods with low or moderate poverty (see Figure 5, p.13). In fact, African American students from neighborhoods

FIGURE 2

Preschool students have average absence rates above 10 percent, but students in kindergarten and the early elementary grades have lower absence rates

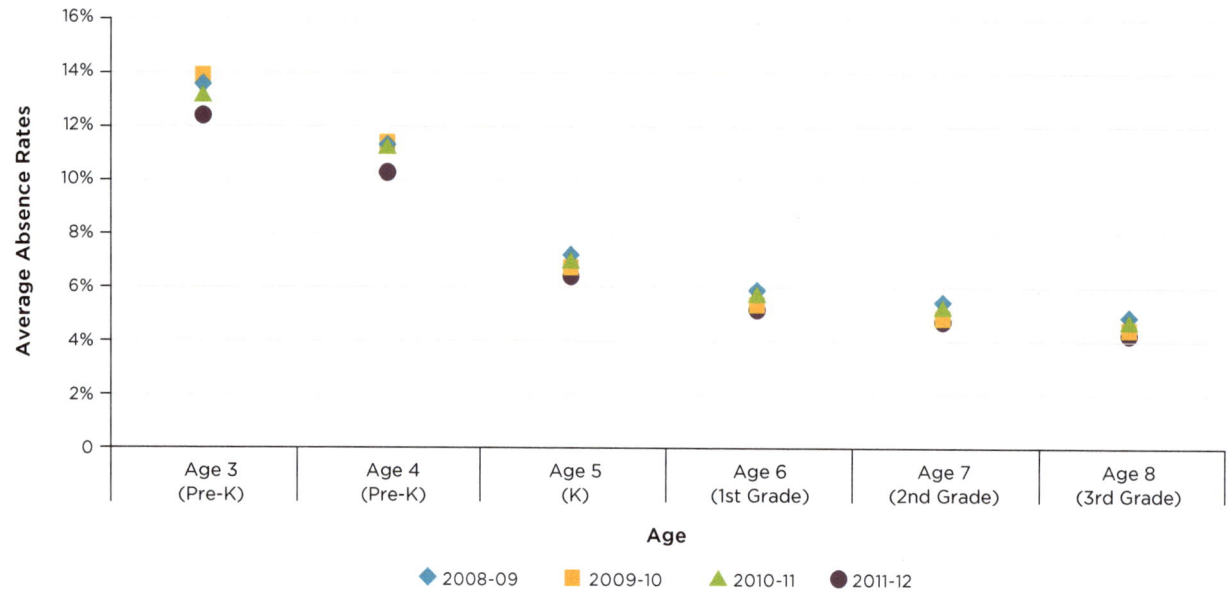

**Note:** Figure 2 shows average absence rates for students, by age, during each of four school years; thus, different ages represent different students (it is a cross-sectional look). But the same pattern shown here, an improvement in attendance after preschool, also exists when we follow the same students over time, from preschool into kindergarten and beyond. In a separate analysis of students who were three years old, in 2008-09, their average absence rates through 2011-12 were as follows: 13.8 percent at age three, 11.5 percent at age four (2009-10), 8.4 percent at age five (2010-11), and 5.2 percent at age six (2011-12).

FIGURE 3

Forty-five percent of three-year-old and 36 percent of four-year-old preschoolers are chronically absent; the rate of chronic absenteeism decreases substantially when children enter kindergarten

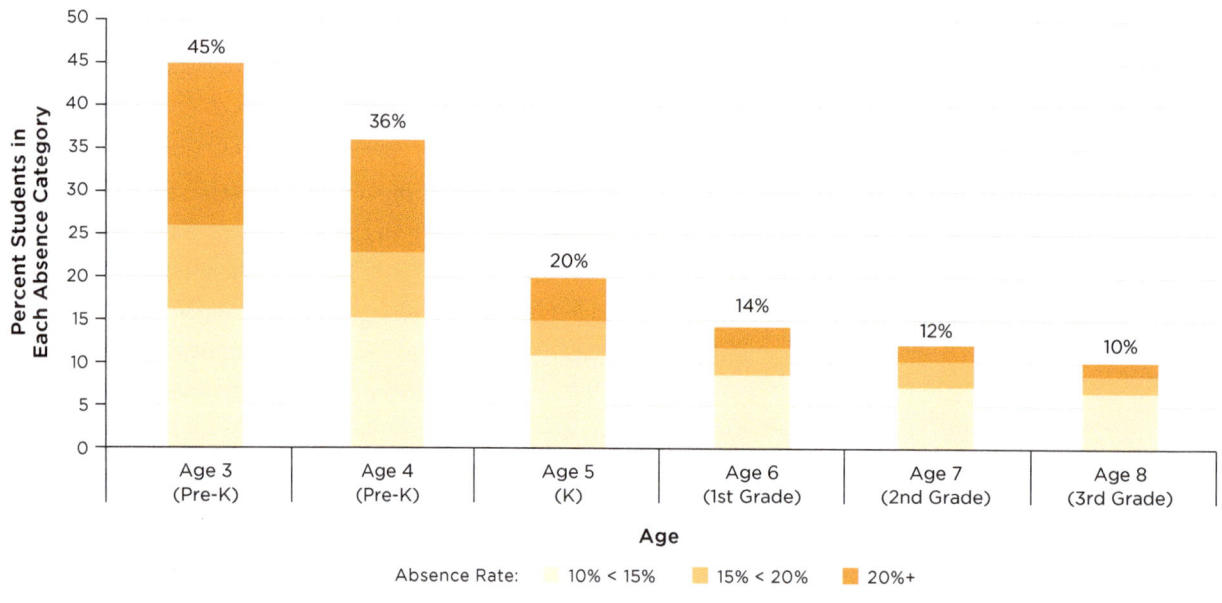

**Note:** Data are from 2011-12; Ns by age group: age three=8,830; age four=16,118; age five=30,598; age six=30,746; age seven=30,736; age eight=27,722.

## Defining Attendance

A number of terms are frequently used to describe student attendance. Schools and programs are often held accountable for their **average daily attendance**, which is the average percentage of enrolled students who attend school each day. Although the average attendance rate for a program is a useful measure for looking at improvement over time, this metric can mask some nuances of attendance. Take, for example, a group of 100 students in a school with an overall average attendance rate of 95 percent. Several different scenarios can result in the same overall attendance rate for this school. In one case, each student misses 5 percent of school, equally contributing to the overall attendance rate of 95 percent. Alternatively, it could be the case that the 20 students each miss 25 percent of school days while all other students show up every day of the year, also resulting in an overall attendance rate of 95 percent for the school. These two scenarios—in which the overall attendance rate is the same—can mean very different things for individual students. In the first case, all students are missing some school, but no one student is missing a substantial amount. In the second scenario, some students are missing a sizeable amount of school.[D]

Because attendance rates can mask very different attendance patterns for individual students, in this report we focus on attendance at the individual level. A student's **attendance rate** is defined as the number of days a student shows up to school out of the total days that student is enrolled. Students may be enrolled for different numbers of days because some students enter school or leave in the middle of the year. Alternatively, out of the number of days enrolled, **absence rate** is the number of days a student misses school.

We also consider whether students are **chronically absent**, defined here as missing 10 percent or more of school, regardless of the reason for the absence. We use this "cutoff" of 10 percent for several reasons. First, most research on chronic absenteeism with older students uses this definition.[E] Second, we show in Chapter 2 that preschool students who miss at least 10 percent of school have significantly lower kindergarten readiness skills than children who attend school most regularly. Preschool students who miss at least 10 percent of school are also more likely to be chronically absent in future years.

In some instances (**see Chapter 3**), we categorized students into six groups based on their absence rates (**shown in Table 2**). The first three categories, also used in other attendance research,[F] differentiate among students who are not chronically absent — those who are absent less than 10 percent of the time. Because absence rates are so high among preschool children, we added three additional categories to differentiate among students who are chronically absent.

The definition of chronic absenteeism is distinct from truancy, which signals the potential need for legal intervention under state compulsory education laws. Truancy rates only include absences that are unexcused; chronic absenteeism does not differentiate between excused and unexcused absences because both result in a day of missed learning.

**TABLE 2**

**Definitions of absence categories used in this report and the corresponding days missed over the full school year.**

| Category | Absence Rates | Maximum Days Missed Based on Full Preschool Year (150 days) |
|---|---|---|
| 1 | 0%<3.3% | 5 days (~1 week) |
| 2 | 3.3%<6.6% | 10 days (~2 weeks) |
| 3 | 6.6%<10% | 15 days (~3 weeks) |
| 4 | 10%<15% | 22.5 days (~4.5 weeks) |
| 5 | 15%<20% | 30 days (~6 weeks) |
| 6 | 20% + | >6 weeks |

**Note:** In CPS preschool programs from 2008-09 through 2011-12, the full school year was approximately 150 school days. This is fewer than the full school year for students in kindergarten through twelfth grade, for whom the school year was 170 days; the difference can be accounted for by the higher number of professional development days allotted for preschool teachers.

## Absence Rates over the School Year

Students miss more school at certain times of the year (**see Figure 4**). Absences are most prevalent in the winter months: on average, children miss three percentage points more school in the winter months than when school first starts (about 11.5 percent of school in January compared with 8.1 percent in September). During the spring, absence rates are somewhat better than during the winter—dropping to about 10.2 percent—but they never return to levels seen at the beginning of the year. This suggests that encouragement for regular attendance needs to occur not only at the beginning of the year but also as the school year progresses.

### Patterns in Absences

We wondered whether students with similar absence rates might exhibit different patterns of absences, in terms of missing a day here and there or missing large blocks of days at a time. For example, one student may miss a day or two each month and have an overall absence rate of 10 percent, while another student might have one long absence episode (e.g., to visit family in another country) and also end up with a 10 percent absence rate. One might speculate that these different patterns are related to children's learning in distinct ways. Perhaps, a student who misses one long stretch of time has a better chance of catching back up in school when s/he returns after the absence, compared to peers who miss for shorter lengths of time more frequently. On the other hand, it may be harder for a student to recover from one long absence. Either way, absence patterns have the potential to be related to learning outcomes. Because we explore the relationship between absences and outcomes in the next chapter, here we examine whether there was evidence that children displayed different patterns of attendance.

To explore patterns in absences, we used cluster analysis on a sample of almost 19,000 three- and four-year-old students in 2010-11, categorizing students into groups based on two aspects of their absences: (1) the number of absence **incidents** a student had over the school year, and (2) the length of each student's longest absence from school Our analyses revealed that, in general, these two variables were strongly related to each other and also to a student's overall absence rate.[G] Students who ever missed a long period of school also had many incidences of absences throughout the year. In other words, it was uncommon for children to miss a single, lengthy period of time without also having other smaller incidents of absence. This means that students with higher absence rates throughout this report were likely to be missing school both more frequently and for longer periods of time than students with lower absence rates.[H]

**FIGURE 4**

**Absence rates are highest during the winter months**

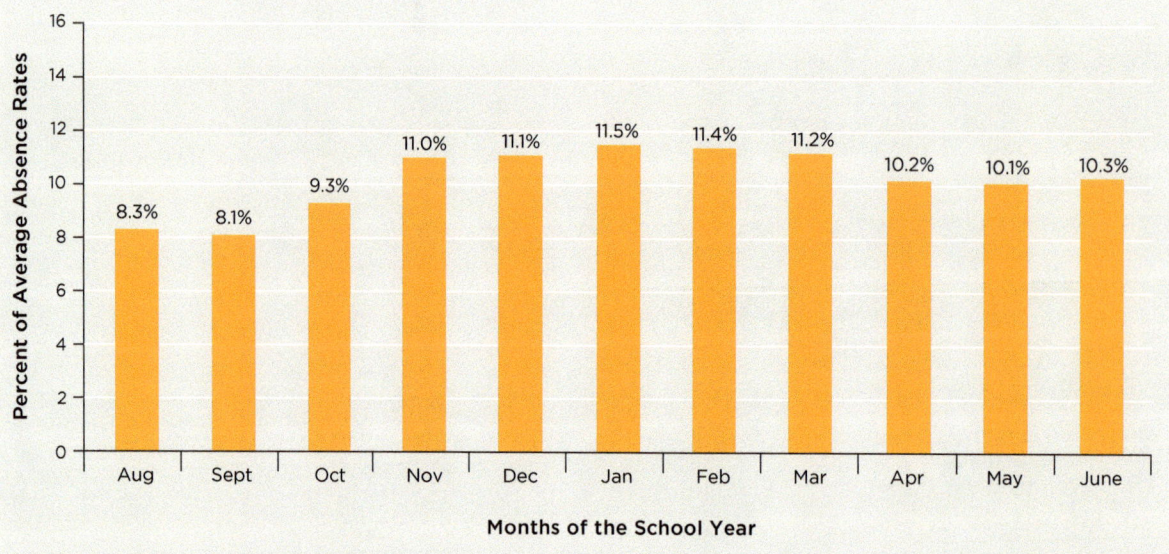

**Note:** Data are from 2011-12; N=25,279.

**FIGURE 5**

African American students are more likely to be chronically absent than students of other racial/ethnic backgrounds, regardless of poverty level.

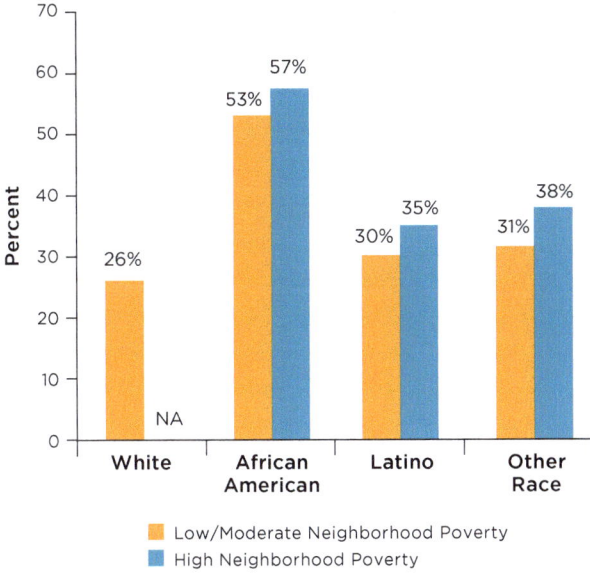

**Note:** (1) This figure is based on three- and four-year olds from 2011-12; N=24,854. There were not enough white students living in high-poverty neighborhoods to include their absence rates on this figure (n<30). (2) The category "Other Race" includes: Native American/Alaskan Native, Asian/Pacific Islander, Pacific Islander/Hawaiian, and Multicultural. (3) There were no significant differences between absence rates in low- vs. moderate-poverty neighborhoods, so they are collapsed here. Poverty is based on the unemployment and income levels in a student's residential block group.

with low or moderate poverty are more likely to be chronically absent than Latino students living in high-poverty neighborhoods. Chapter 3 explores in greater depth the reasons why African American preschool students miss more school than white or Latino students.

Although race is most strongly associated with absenteeism, poverty does still have a significant relationship with chronically absenteeism. Students of all races/ethnicities are more likely to be chronically absent if they live in neighborhoods with substantial levels of poverty. However, the differences in chronic absenteeism between high-poverty neighborhoods and low/moderate-poverty neighborhoods for students of a given race/ethnicity are more modest than differences between racial/ethnic groups.

Given that absenteeism is more prevalent among African Americans, it is not surprising that preschools with the highest average absence rates are located in neighborhoods that are predominantly African American. **Figure 6** shows that across Chicago, schools with the lowest average preschool attendance (highest average absence rates) are clustered in neighborhoods with higher proportions of African American residents. However, there are also examples across the city where two schools that are located very close to each other—often serving similar populations of students—look very different in terms of their preschool attendance rates. In Chapter 3, we explore whether there are school context factors that explain attendance patterns after taking into account the population of students being served.

In addition to race and poverty, several other background characteristics were also related to the likelihood of being chronically absent during preschool. Four-year-olds were less likely to be chronically absent than three-year-olds. Four-year-olds who attended a CPS preschool program in the prior year, when they were three years old, were less likely to be chronically absent than those who were not CPS preschoolers the previous year. English Language Learners (ELL) were also less likely to be chronically absent than students who were not ELL. Other characteristics, such as gender and receiving special education services, were not associated with differences in chronic absenteeism.[16]

FIGURE 6

**Schools with higher preschool absence rates are clustered in predominantly African American neighborhoods, but some schools have better attendance rates than expected given neighborhood characteristics**

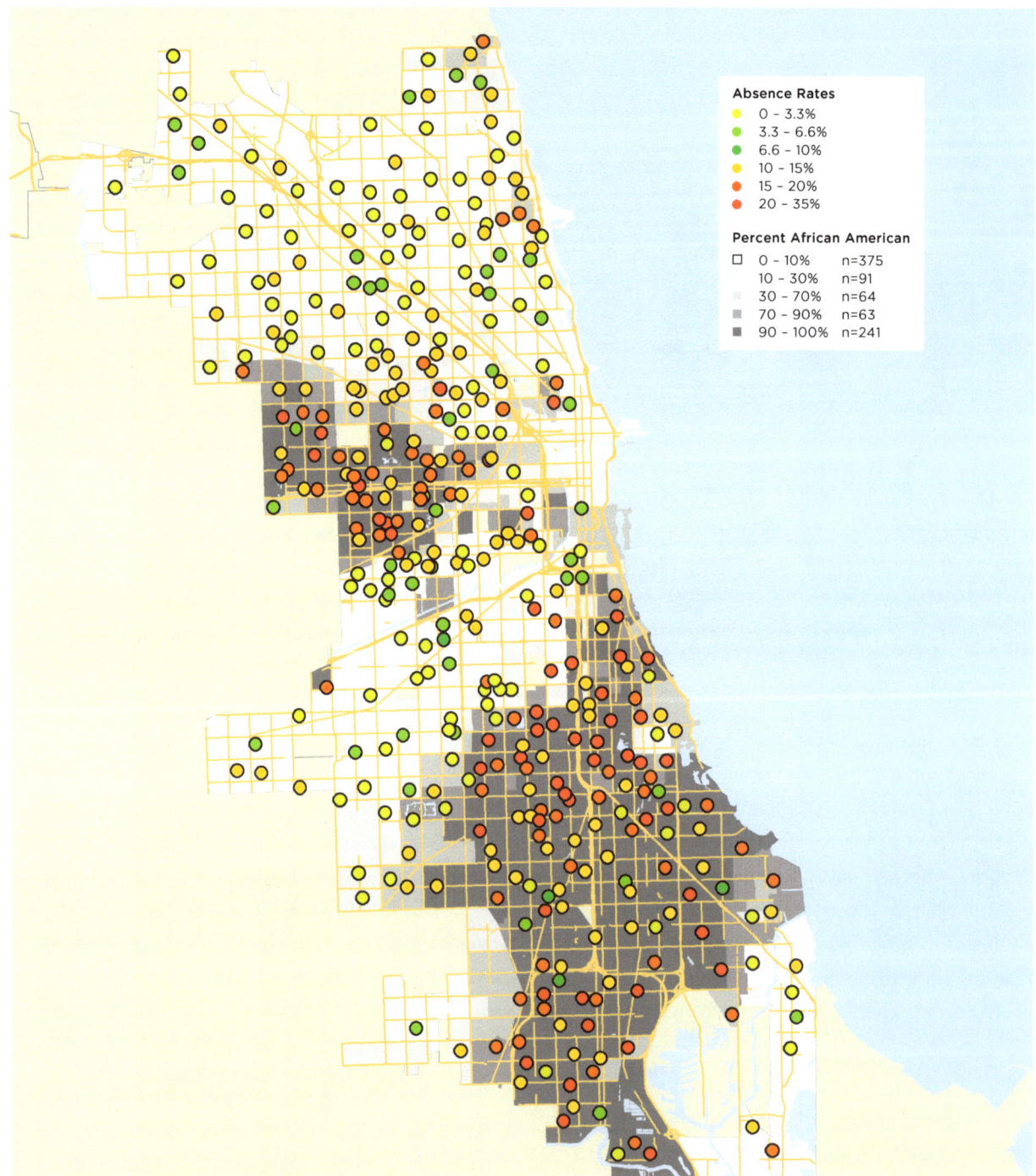

### HOW TO READ FIGURE 6

Each circle represents a school, and the colors correspond to the average absence rate for their preschool students. The grey tones in the background depict the proportion of the population that is African American, by census block.

## Summary

Chronic absenteeism among preschool students in CPS is extremely high; about 40 percent of all preschoolers miss 10 percent or more of school, or at least 15 days for a student enrolled for the entire school year. However, attendance improves substantially as children move into kindergarten and the early elementary grades. African American students are the most likely to be chronically absent, and living in a high-poverty neighborhood also increases a student's chances of being chronically absent. Given the prevalence of chronic absenteeism among preschool students, the next chapter explores whether missing a lot of school has any implications for students' learning outcomes, both during preschool and in the early elementary grades.

CHAPTER 2

# Preschool Attendance and Primary Grade Outcomes

Preschool attendance is significantly related to student outcomes, both at the end of preschool and in later years. CPS students with more absences during preschool had lower skills as measured by a kindergarten readiness assessment—even when we take into account their skill level when they started preschool. Better attendance was more beneficial for students who entered preschool with the lowest academic skills; unfortunately, these were also the students most likely to be chronically absent.

Although attendance improves substantially between preschool and kindergarten, chronic absenteeism remains a significant problem for some students throughout the elementary grades. In fact, students who miss many days of preschool are much more likely than other students to continue this pattern into kindergarten and beyond. Students with successive years of chronic absenteeism from preschool into the early elementary years not only tend to start out with the lowest skills but also continue to fall behind their classmates. At the end of second grade, students with multiple years of chronic absenteeism are, on average, in need of reading interventions.

## Is Preschool Attendance Related to Kindergarten Readiness Outcomes?

**Students who miss more preschool have lower kindergarten readiness scores.**
Four-year-olds in CPS who missed more school during the course of a year had lower levels of kindergarten readiness by the end of that year than students who missed fewer days of school (**see Figure 7, p.19**). As absence rates increased, students' scores decreased on all four subscales of the KRT: math, letter recognition, pre-literacy, and social-emotional development. Significant differences on the pre-literacy subscale emerged for students who missed at least 6.6 percent of school days, compared with students with the best attendance (absence rate between 0 and 3.3 percent). On the math, letter recognition, and social-emotional subscales, students who missed 10 percent or more of school had significantly lower scores than students with the best attendance.

The scale in **Figure 7** uses logit units (which is not an intuitively meaningful unit, although it provides a constant comparison across subscales). An alternative way to think about how strongly attendance is related to learning outcomes is to compare the percent of items students correctly answered on each KRT subscale by different levels of attendance. In math, the students with the best attendance correctly answered 88 percent of the questions, on average, compared to 82 percent correctly answered by students who missed between 10 and 15 percent of school, and 75 percent for students who missed at least 20 percent of school. Differences across attendance levels were largest on the letter recognition subscale; regular attenders knew about 90 percent of the letters and sounds assessed, while students who missed between 10 and 15 percent of school knew only 84 percent, and those who missed the most school only knew about 68 percent. This subscale of the KRT constitutes the very basic literacy knowledge students will need for success in kindergarten and beyond. There were smaller differences in outcomes by attendance levels on the pre-literacy subscale: Students in the highest and lowest attendance groups scored about eight percentage points apart.[17] Importantly, attendance was not only related to academic outcomes, but also to social-emotional outcomes. Students who missed more school were rated by their teachers as having lower levels of appropriate behavior and work habits.

Students start preschool with different levels of prior skills and backgrounds, and this can contribute to differences in their performance on the KRT at the end of the year. Indeed, in our sample, students who missed more preschool were also the students who began the year with the lowest skills (**see Table A.3 on p.45 in Appendix A**).[18] However, even after taking into account test scores at the beginning of the year and background characteristics, missing more school was

> ## Data Used to Study the Relationship between Preschool Attendance and Preschool Achievement Outcomes
>
> ### Sample
> Our analysis examining the relationship between absenteeism in preschool and kindergarten readiness at the end of preschool used a sample of 1,265 four-year-old students who were part of CPS's Preschool Longitudinal Study (PLS) in 2010-11. Students in this sample were not exactly equivalent to the overall preschool population; they were more likely to be white and less likely to be Latino or receiving special education services than the full four-year-old CPS population in 2010-11 (**see Table A.3 on p.45 in Appendix A**).[i] They were slightly more likely to be from a high-poverty neighborhood, with 16 percent of the PLS sample coming from such neighborhoods compared to 13 percent of all four-year-old students.
>
> ### Achievement Measures
> Students who were part of the PLS sample were administered the Woodcock-Johnson III at the beginning of their preschool year (Fall 2010). They also were administered the CPS-developed Kindergarten Readiness Tool (KRT; in use from 2009 through 2012) as part of a district-wide assessment of kindergarten readiness at the end of the year. We supplemented this achievement data with administrative data received from CPS.
>
> **Woodcock-Johnson III (WJ)**
> The Woodcock-Johnson III is a norm-referenced test that is comprised of many subtests.[j] We use students' Letter-Word Identification scores as a measure of their incoming skills at the beginning of their four-year-old preschool year. This subtest assesses students' ability to identify letters in large print and pronounce words (if they progress far enough into the assessment).
>
> **CPS Kindergarten Readiness Tool (KRT)**
> The Kindergarten Readiness Tool (KRT) consists of 86 items that were administered one-on-one to students by their teacher, and eight items filled out by teachers, during the spring of the preschool year before kindergarten. We identified four subscales on the KRT: math, letter recognition, pre-literacy, and social-emotional development. See Appendix B for a description of Rasch analyses on the KRT that were used to identify subscales.
>
> - The **math** subscale assesses students on basic number concepts, comparisons and ordinal numbers, geometry and measurement, sorting, and addition/subtraction problem solving skills.
> - **Letter recognition** consists of a set of items that require children to identify the names and sounds of individual letters.
> - **Pre-literacy** focuses on phonics and phonological awareness, print awareness, oral story-telling, and comprehension.
> - The **social-emotional development** subscale is comprised of eight items filled out by students' teachers that assess student behavior and work habits.
>
> For a more detailed description of data sources, samples, and analyses, see Appendix A.

still significantly associated with lower scores in math, letter recognition, and social-emotional development, as shown by the light-colored bars in **Figure 7**. In other words, some differences seen across children at the end of the year are because they started the year with varying levels of incoming skills, but some differences are related to their attendance. Among students with similar incoming skills and backgrounds, students who missed 10 percent or more of school—those considered chronically absent—still performed significantly worse on the math and letter recognition portions of the KRT than students who had the best attendance. For social-emotional outcomes, a significant difference emerged between students who missed at least 20 percent of school compared with those who missed the least amount of school.[19] For pre-literacy outcomes, once we took into account children's letter recognition skills at the beginning of the year, there was no significant relationship between attendance and end-of-year scores. Some students started the year with higher skills in this domain and they maintained that advantage over other students who started the year with lower pre-literacy skills, regardless of their attendance. Taken together, these findings show CPS students who entered preschool at age four with the lowest skills were the most likely to exhibit high absenteeism during the course of the year, ultimately ending preschool with the lowest levels of academic and social-emotional skills.

## FIGURE 7

Four year-olds who miss more preschool perform worse on kindergarten readiness measures of math, letter recognition, and social-emotional development at the end of their year, even after controlling for incoming skills and background characteristics

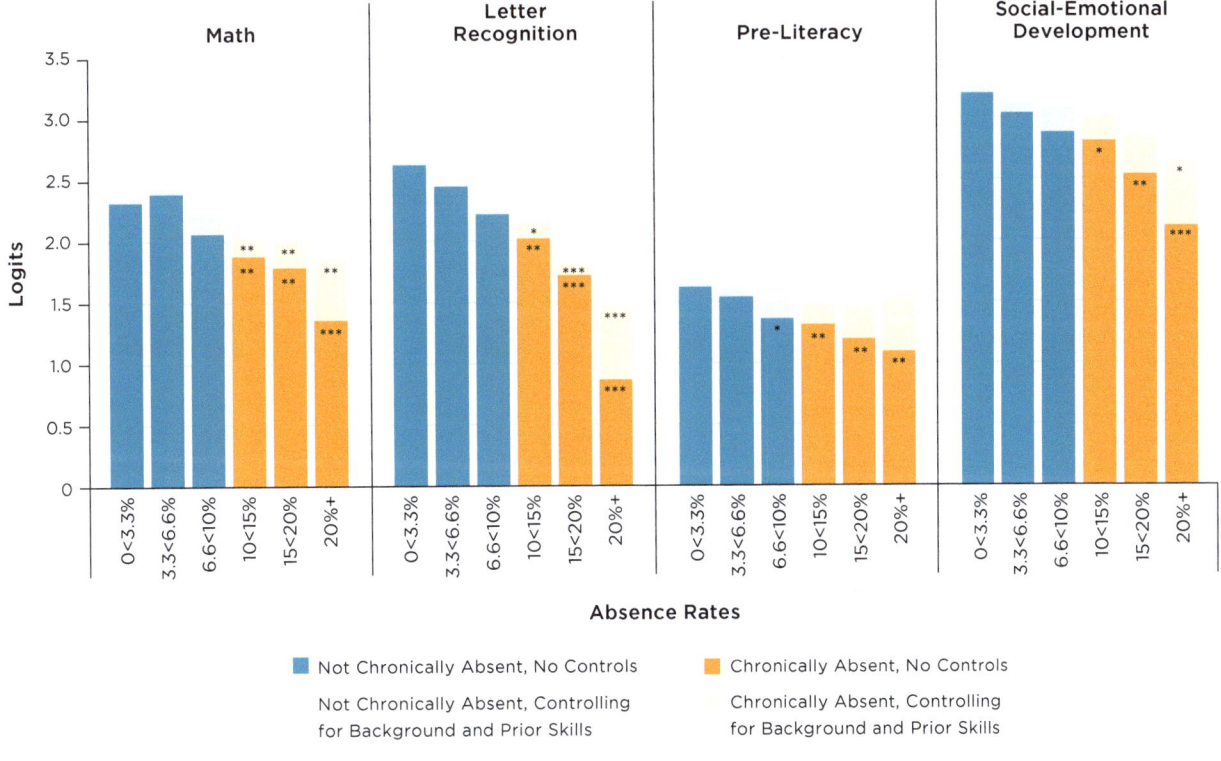

**Note:** (1) The sample for these analyses include four-year-old students who took both the Woodcock-Johnson III at the beginning of the school year and the KRT at the end of the school year in 2010-11 (n=1,265); * $p<.05$; ** $p<.01$; *** $p<.001$.

### HOW TO READ FIGURE 7

This figure shows average scores on the four KRT subscales for students in each of six attendance categories (**described in *Defining "Attendance"* on p.11**). The **BLUE** bars represent children who are not chronically absent, while the **YELLOW** bars represent chronically absent children. The **DARKER BLUE** and **YELLOW** bars show average KRT scores without taking into account background characteristics and incoming Woodcock-Johnson III Letter-Word Identification scores. The **LIGHTER BLUE** and **YELLOW** bars show average scores after taking these factors into account (i.e., race/ethnicity, gender, special education status, English Language Learner status, whether student was in preschool the prior year, neighborhood poverty status, neighborhood social status, and incoming WJ III Letter-Word Identification scores). Background characteristics and WJ III scores have been centered on the average value for students with the best attendance (absences between 0 and 3.3 percent), so that the light yellow and blue bars are the expected scores for students in each category if they had the *same characteristics and incoming skills as students in the lowest absence category.* The difference between the top of the dark bars and the top of the light bars is the portion of KRT scores that can be attributed to differences in incoming skills and background characteristics. Scores are measured in logits, which are not intuitively meaningful. However, the height of the bars can be compared across outcomes: Students' scores are highest on the social-emotional component of the KRT and lowest on the pre-literacy component. The lower asterisks indicate that scores are significantly different from those of students with absences between 0% and 3.3% without taking into account background characteristics and incoming skills. The higher asterisks indicate that scores are significantly different from those of students with absences between 0 and 3.3 percent after taking these factors into account.

**Good attendance is related to greater academic gains for students with lower incoming skills.**
As shown above, attendance is related to preschool students' learning and behavioral outcomes. However, attendance is more strongly related to math and letter recognition for students who entered preschool with the weakest skills than among students who entered preschool with the strongest skills (**see Figure 8**).[20] Differences in the relationships between attendance and KRT scores for students by incoming skill level were most notable on students' letter recognition scores.[21] For example, among students who entered with low levels of prior skills, the difference in letter recognition scores for students who missed 3.3 percent of school compared to students who missed 15 percent of school was 0.66 logits. Among students who entered with high prior skills, the difference in scores between these two groups was 0.11 logits. **Appendix C** describes a similar analysis looking at growth on the same test over time.

**FIGURE 8**

The relationship between attendance and learning outcomes in math and letter recognition is strongest for students who enter school with lower skills.

**Note:** (1) The sample for these analyses include four-year-old students who took both the Woodcock-Johnson III at the beginning of the school year and the KRT at the end of the school year in 2010-11 (n=1,265). (2) Main effects of absence rate on KRT scores are significant at $p<.05$ for math, letter recognition, and social-emotional development subtests. Interaction effects between absence rate and incoming skills on KRT scores are significant at $p<.05$ for math and letter recognition subtests, with an effect size of 0.06 and 0.10 respectively. (3) Students with low levels of prior skills scored 1 standard deviation below the mean on the Woodcock-Johnson III Letter-Word identification and students with high levels of prior skills scored 1 standard deviation above the mean. (4) Because fewer than 10 percent of all children with high prior skills had absence rates higher than 15 percent, we exclude this point estimate from the graphs.

### HOW TO READ FIGURE 8

This figure shows average math, letter recognition, and social-emotional development scores for students who entered preschool with low, average, and high levels of incoming skills. Scores are calculated from a statistical model in which we controlled for background characteristics and incoming achievement (i.e., race/ethnicity, gender, special education status, English Language Learner status, whether student was in preschool the prior year, neighborhood poverty status, neighborhood social status, and incoming Woodcock-Johnson III Letter Identification scores). The **YELLOW** line represents students who entered preschool with the highest skills, the **GREEN** line represents children who entered preschool with average skills, and the **BLUE** line represents students who entered with the lowest incoming skills. The lines show the relationship between absenteeism and KRT outcomes for each of these groups of students. The steepest line—that of students with the lowest incoming skills—means that the difference in learning outcomes between those who attend school regularly and those who miss 20 percent or more of preschool is the largest for this group of students.

It may be the case that students who enter preschool with higher skill levels learn their numbers and letters at home, so that missing school does not have as strong an impact on their academic skills. For students who enter preschool with low skill levels, preschool may be particularly important for learning letter recognition and math, as their home experiences did not lead them to have strong skills when they entered preschool.[22] For these students, attending school regularly seems to be particularly important, given that they start off so much further behind other students.

As for students' social-emotional learning, there were no differences in the relationship between attendance and learning based on prior skills. For all students, better attendance was equally related to better social-emotional outcomes, regardless of skill level.

## Is Preschool Attendance Related to Later Attendance and Learning Outcomes?

Chronically absent preschool students are five times more likely to be chronically absent in kindergarten. Not only are chronically absent preschool students more likely to enter kindergarten with lower skill levels than their non-chronically absent peers but they also are more likely to be chronically absent in kindergarten and beyond. Around one-third of students who were chronically absent in preschool were still chronically absent in kindergarten (see Figure 9). By comparison, only seven percent of non-chronically absent preschool students were chronically absent in kindergarten. The higher a student's absence rate was in preschool, the more likely s/he was to continue being chronically

**FIGURE 9**

One-third of chronically absent four-year-olds continue to be chronically absent in kindergarten; of those students, more than 30 percent are still chronically absent in second grade.

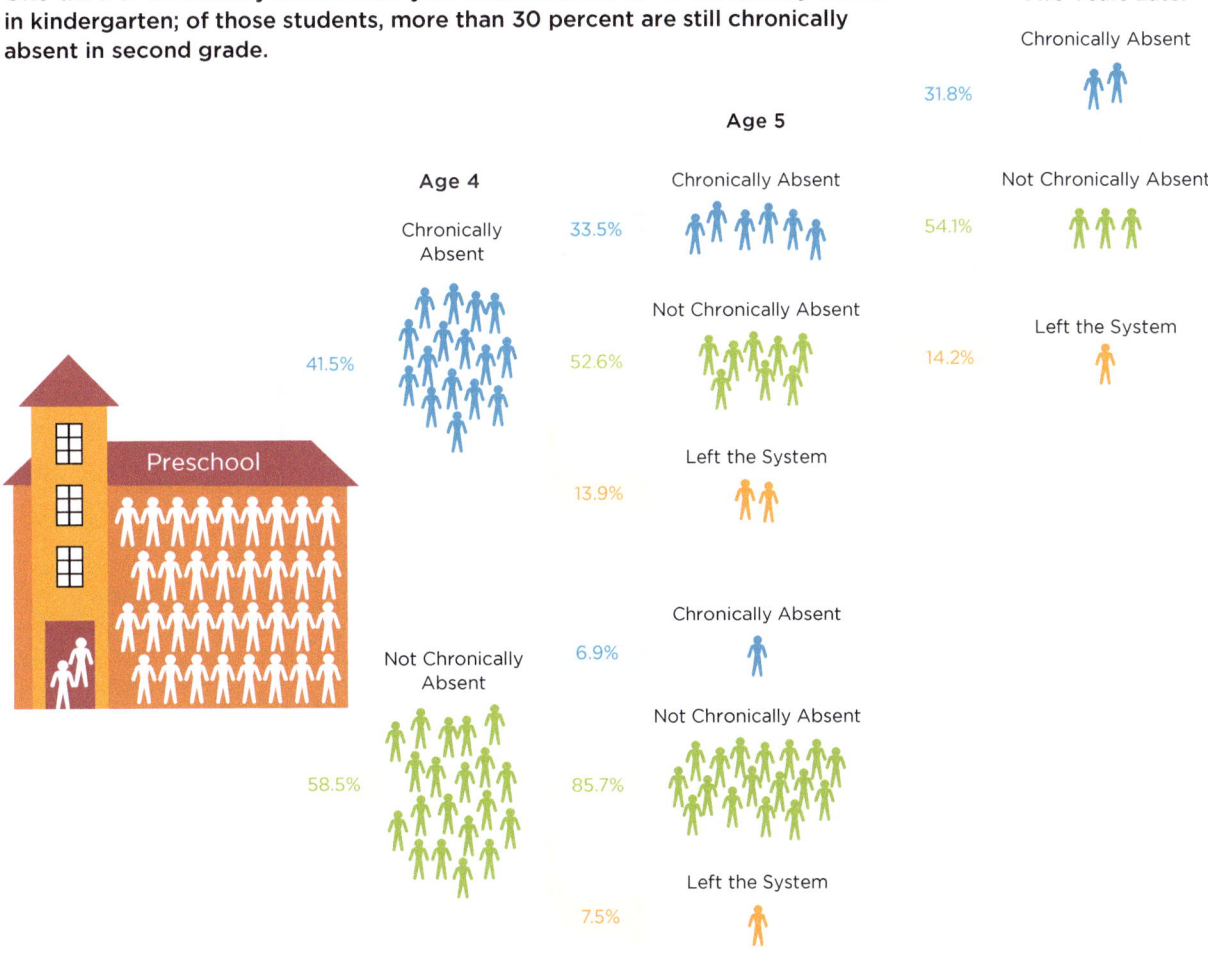

**Note:** Population includes students who were in preschool at age 4 in 2008-09; n=15,713

absent in kindergarten. Students who missed at least 20 percent of preschool were the most likely to be chronically absent in kindergarten; almost 60 percent of these students were still chronically absent in second grade, compared with less than 30 percent of students who were absent between 10 and 20 percent in preschool. However, both groups of students were likely to be among those chronically absent in kindergarten.[23] Thus, it is important to carefully monitor all chronically absent preschool students as they enter kindergarten to break the pattern of missing extensive amounts of school.

This relationship between chronic absenteeism in preschool and kindergarten continues on to second grade: The more that students miss preschool, the greater their odds of being chronically absent in second grade (see Table 3). In fact, students who are chronically absent in preschool are five times more likely to be chronically absent in second grade (3.1 vs. 15.5 percent). While there is a relationship between preschool and second grade attendance, a more accurate picture of who will exhibit continued struggles with attendance into the elementary years forms when children's attendance is monitored in both preschool and kindergarten; students who are chronically absent in both years are at elevated risk of chronic absenteeism in first and second grade. One-third of all students who are chronically absent in both preschool and kindergarten are still chronically absent in second grade (see Figure 9).

**Multiple Years of Chronic Absenteeism are Linked to Significantly Lower Second Grade Reading Scores.**
Students who were chronically absent for multiple years between preschool and second grade had significantly lower test scores by the end of second grade than students who were not chronically absent over multiple years. **Figure 10** shows DIBELS Oral Reading Fluency (ORF) scores for students based on the number of years they were chronically absent between preschool and second grade, without taking into account prior achievement.[24,25] Students who were chronically absent in both preschool and kindergarten, but not chronically absent after that, had reading fluency scores indicating they were at-risk for needing reading intervention. Students who were chronically absent all four years between preschool and second grade had reading fluency scores that were, on average, close to the benchmark for being at risk for *substantial* reading intervention.[26] This means that many students in this group are in need of intensive reading intervention before they even enter third grade. In fact, 44 percent of students who were chronically absent all four years had DIBELS scores suggesting they were in need of intensive intervention, and another 18 percent had scores indicating a need of some reading supports. This is concerning given research showing that children who are not reading at grade level by the end of third grade have ongoing academic and social-emotional struggles.[27] Just over 4 percent of all students who were in the CPS system from preschool through second grade fall into this group of students who were chronically absent in all four years.[28]

**TABLE 3**

**The likelihood of being chronically absent through second grade is related to students' preschool absence rates**

| Level of Absenteeism in Preschool | Percent Chronically Absent in Kindergarten | Percent Chronically Absent in Second Grade |
|---|---|---|
| 0<3.3% | 3.9% | 2.4% |
| 3.3<6.6% | 6.6% | 3.0% |
| 6.6<10% | 12.5% | 5.7% |
| 10<15% | 22.8% | 11.1% |
| 15<20% | 36.5% | 18.6% |
| 20+% | 58.5% | 31.0% |

**Note:** Analyses follow all four-year-olds in 2008-09 who have available data in either 2009-10 for kindergarten (n = 14,119) and/or 2011-12 for second grade (n = 12,891).

**FIGURE 10**

The more years students are chronically absent in the early years, the more at-risk they are for needing reading interventions by the end of second grade

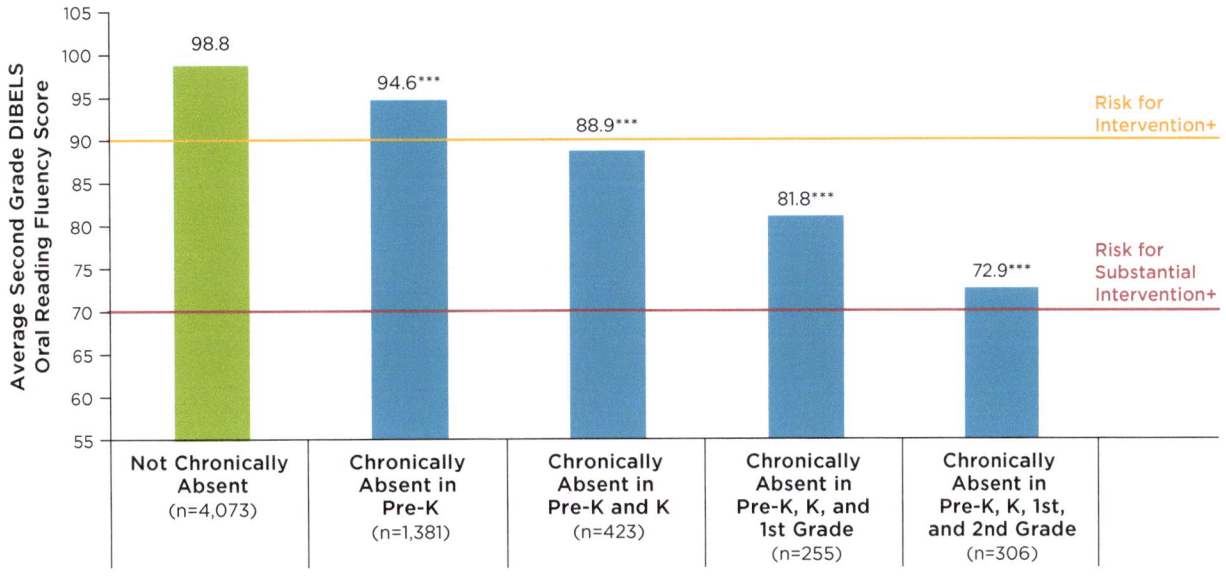

**Note:** ***Indicates that scores are significantly different from scores of students who are never chronically absent, at p<.001 level.

+ In the DIBELS 6th Edition Assessment and Scoring Guide (Good & Kaminksi, 2002), these are labeled as "Some Risk," indicating the need for additional intervention and "At Risk," indicating the need for substantial interventions.

### HOW TO READ FIGURE 10

The **GREEN BAR** on the far left represents students who never were chronically absent between preschool and second grade. The first **BLUE BAR** denotes students who were chronically absent in preschool but no other years; the next denotes students who were chronically absent in both preschool and kindergarten, but no other years; and so on. The significance notation indicates that students represented in that bar performed significantly worse on the DIBELS than students who were never chronically absent over the four years. The analysis is based on a sample of 7,236 students who were in preschool in 2008-09 and in second grade in 2011-12. Not all combinations of chronic absence are shown here.

## Data Used to Study the Relationship between Attendance and Second Grade Outcomes

### Sample

Our analyses examining the relationship between attendance and second-grade outcomes focused on a sample of 7,236 students who were four years old in 2008-09 and were also given the DIBELS in 2011-12 as second-graders. (**See Appendix A** for full description of the sample and analysis.) Students in CPS are not required to take assessments until they are in third grade. However, a large number of schools use the DIBELS ORF to assess reading accuracy and fluency at the end of second grade. As of 2011-12, when we examined this outcome, charter schools either did not administer the DIBELS in their schools or did not report those scores to CPS.

The sample used in this analysis was very similar to the full population from which it was drawn (**see Table A.4 on p.47 in Appendix A**). They represent 46 percent of all four-year-old preschool students in 2008-09. The sample was similar in background characteristics to the full four-year-old population, except that the DIBELS-takers were slightly less likely to be African American (perhaps a function of the fact that charter schools did not administer the DIBELS or provide that data to CPS).

### Achievement Measure: Dynamic Indicators of Basic Early Literacy Skills—Oral Reading Fluency (DIBELS ORF)

DIBELS ORF is a standardized reading fluency assessment designed for use with students between first and third grade. Students are given a text to read through and are scored based on how quickly and accurately they read that text out loud. Students with a score of 90 or above at the end of second grade are considered to be reading at grade level.[K] Those who score between 70 and 89 are at some risk for needing intervention, while those who score below 70 likely need intensive interventions.

**For a more detailed description of data sources, samples, and analyses, see Appendix A.**

## Summary

Students with higher preschool absence rates had lower academic outcomes at the end of preschool than students with lower absence rates, even after controlling for their incoming skills. Significant differences appeared between students who regularly attended school and those who were chronically absent (missing 10 percent or more days of school). Students with higher absences also tended to start preschool with lower levels of incoming skills, on average. These students—those who started the year furthest behind and missed substantial amounts of school—failed to narrow the achievement gap as much as their peers who attended school more frequently. Preschool attendance can also be an early indicator for future attendance problems, particularly for students who are chronically absent in both preschool and kindergarten. These students are especially vulnerable to lower learning outcomes by the end of second grade, and many need reading supports by this early time in their educational career. Given the importance early attendance plays in students' educational trajectories and outcomes, the next chapter turns to better understanding why preschool students miss so much school.

CHAPTER 3

# Reasons for Preschool Absences

The high rates of chronic preschool absenteeism in Chicago are due mainly to a range of health and logistical obstacles. Particular family circumstances can further exacerbate these obstacles. For example, logistical challenges are more difficult to overcome if only one parent in the home can provide transportation; parents with poor health face more struggles getting their children to school, as do families who rely on public transportation. How regularly children attend preschool is also related to parents' beliefs about the importance of preschool; parents who believe preschool attendance is very important and sets the stage for good attendance later, have children who attend more often. Finally, preschool attendance is related to several aspects of school climate. Attendance is better in schools where teachers feel safe and more connected to the school as a whole. Attendance is also better in schools where teachers share a strong sense of school commitment, trust with parents is strong, and parent involvement is high.

## Why Are Preschool Students Absent?

Sickness and logistical obstacles are the most common reasons for absences.

Based on attendance logs from 57 classrooms over a nine-week period, sickness was the most common reason preschool children missed school (**see Figure 11**). Just over half of days missed (54 percent) were for reasons including the flu, a cold, ear infections, or other non-chronic illness. Three percent of missed days were due specifically to a chronic illness, most often asthma. An additional 4 percent of absences were because children had a wellness appointment, such as a check-up, the dentist, or therapy.

Children were also absent because of a range of obstacles, including transportation, child care, and an array of family-related reasons. These account for 18 percent of absences and are represented by the green slices in **Figure 11**. Some families had difficulty getting their

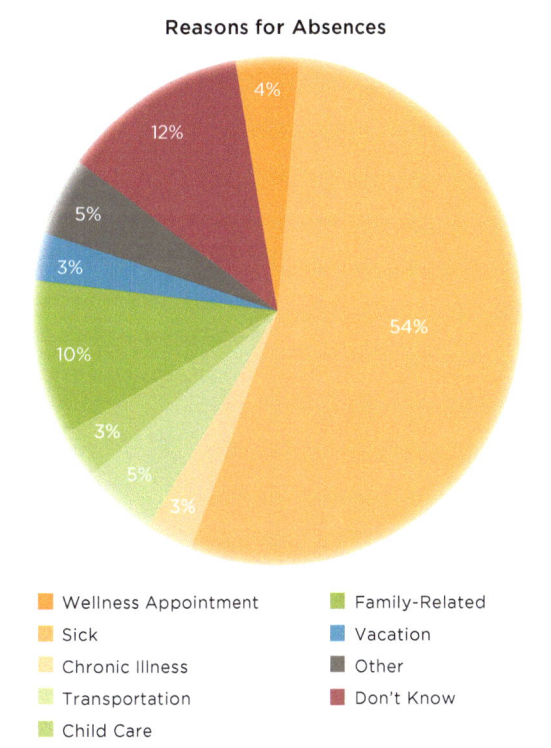

**FIGURE 11**

Sickness accounts for just over half of all days missed from school, while transportation, child care, and family-related reasons account for another 18 percent of days missed

**Data Source:** Attendance logs; n = 1,229

child to and from school, particularly given the half-day schedule of many programs. Families also had to work around child care arrangements, which sometimes did not align well with school hours (**see *The Struggle of the Half-Day Schedule* on p.26**). For example, one parent interviewed described how she did not always have someone to take her child to/from school:

> Sometimes [both Luisa's father and I have to] work and we can't work with the [preschool] schedule at work. We have to have her grandparents take care of her…We're kind of further away from our family members and we have no one to come and pick Luisa up.[29]

## The Struggle of the Half-Day Schedule

The vast majority of CPS preschool students in school-based programs are enrolled in half-day programs. In 2011-12, only 56 of 682 classrooms were full-day.[L] For the children in our study, this meant most were attending school for three hours a day, at most. Many of our interviewed parents expressed frustration about the short length of their child's program. About one-third of the parents reported that the short schedule was difficult to plan around. Most parents in this group mentioned that their child occasionally missed school due to the inconvenience of the schedule. The hours conflicted with parent work, with other children's schedules, and/or with the supplemental daycare schedule. The abbreviated schedule created logistical issues for many working parents, and even occasionally caused challenges for parents who had worked out solutions to the scheduling conflicts. One parent said,

> I use transportation from my daycare to pick them up and drop them off, so I really don't have any issues getting them to school or anything like that, until the daycare's closed... On those days, I have to have her stay home because I work, and I can't pick her up at 11:00...She has to stay at home.

During the interview, a number of parents shared how they made the half-day schedule work. Some parents were stay-at-home parents. Others were able to adapt to the schedule because they had flexibility at work or there were two parents in the household who could help out. Parents who lived near their child's school reported that proximity made it easier to juggle their child's school schedule with their own work schedule(s). However, even some parents who stated that the hours/schedule generally worked reported occasionally having trouble getting their child to/from school due to the abbreviated schedule. One parent explained,

> If I had a job interview and I knew that I wasn't gonna be able to pick them up at 2:30 or something, then yeah, they probably [didn't make it to school] 'cause I knew I probably wouldn't have made it back to get them on time. And I wouldn't want to leave my kids sittin' at school, and then have them worry if I wasn't able to pick them back up on time, you know? [So I left them at home with a babysitter.]

The half-day program also played a role in how important parents believed attendance in preschool was for their child's learning. Some parents we interviewed said that attendance in preschool did not matter because their child's preschool program was "only two-and-a-half hours" long. With such a short program, how much could their child be missing if s/he stayed home for the day?

Regardless of whether or not the schedule worked for them, many parents expressed a desire for a longer program. They said that a longer day would set a routine for kindergarten, provide a better foundation for later grades, and provide an opportunity for students to learn more concepts. One parent expressed a concern that the short school day did not provide enough time for learning, stating,

> I think, because of the...program not being long enough for the students, you know, as far as the time and everything...[the program] prepared her to go into kindergarten, but at the same time, I think that...the program isn't long enough for the students to cram all of that information...

Thus, many parents wanted a full-day program to provide their children with more opportunities to learn and become prepared for kindergarten. This sentiment seems to have contributed to some parents' belief that their children's attendance in preschool was less important than it would be in later grades.

Issues that fell under the "family-related" category included another family member being sick (this was most often a parent or sibling), an older sibling not having school that day, the child staying with another parent too far away from the school, the child needing to attend a Women, Infants, and Children (WIC) appointment with their parent, funerals, court appearances, and parents who overslept. Here, one parent explains why her daughter couldn't attend school when her husband was sick:

> [My husband] got ill this year, so there was a timeframe where Leyla couldn't go all the time because [my husband] had a lot of dental surgery to have done. We just moved to Chicago, so we're not…in the position where we have a lot of options for someone else to pick-up and take the kids…I'm working, so [when my husband was sick] Leyla had to miss a day, so that impacted her going [to school].

This example touches on two categories: transportation and family-related. It was often difficult to fully differentiate among transportation, child care, and family-related reasons. Therefore, we consider all of these categories **logistical obstacles**.

Another five percent of absences occurred for *"other"* reasons and 12 percent of absences were unexplained. These also could have been logistical obstacles or illnesses that were not reported to the teacher, or other issues that were not captured in the attendance logs. Teachers were instructed not to press parents for responses if they were hesitant to explain their child's absence.

## Why Do African American and Latino Children Miss More Preschool?

### African American students miss more school than other students.

As we saw in Chapter 1, African American preschool students are more likely to be chronically absent than white or Latino preschool students. Based on attendance log data, African American students missed nearly 16 percent of school over the nine-week period during which attendance logs were collected (**see Figure 12**).

This was twice as often as white students, who missed fewer than 7 percent of days, and 1.4 times more than Latino students, who missed nearly 11 percent of days.

One reason African American preschool students had higher absence rates than white students was that they missed more days due to reported illness.[30] African American students missed almost 8 percent of

#### FIGURE 12

**African American students miss more school because they are sick and because they face more logistical obstacles**

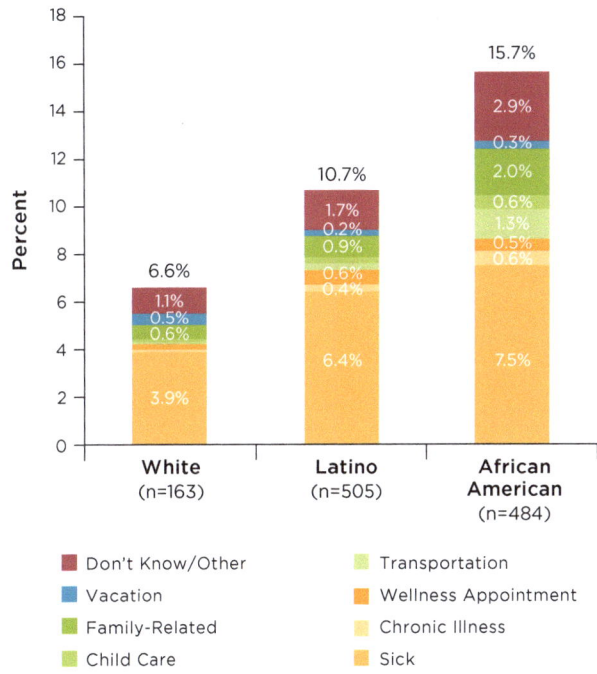

**Data Source:** Attendance logs; n=1,152.

### HOW TO READ FIGURE 12

The total height of each bar represents the overall absence rates of white, Latino, and African American students during the nine-week period in which attendance log data was collected. The subcomponents show how much each reason contributed to the overall absence rate for each group. For example, during this time period African American preschool students missed nearly 16 percent of school, on average. Their absence rate due to chronic and non-chronic illness was around 8 percent (7.5 percent plus 0.6 percent). In other words, if African American preschool students only missed school because they were sick, their absence rate would be 8 percent.

school days because of chronic and non-chronic illness, which was almost twice the rate as white students, who missed about 4 percent of school days because of illness. Illness did not explain much of the difference in attendance rates between African-American and Latino students; Latino students missed about the same amount of school due to illness as African American students—around seven percent of days.

Both African American and Latino students missed more school days because of illness than white students, though nearly all students were likely to become sick at least once during the year. During the nine-week period that log data were collected, around two-thirds of African American, white, and Latino students missed at least one day of school because they were sick (see Figure 13). Thus, students of all races/ethnicities are likely to get sick and miss school at least occasionally during the year. But African American and Latino children missed more often and for longer periods of time than white students, missing nearly twice as many days because of sickness than white students (see Table 4).

While there were only modest differences between African American and Latino students' absences due to illness, African American students differed from Latino

### TABLE 4

Latino and African American students missed more days, on average, due to sickness and logistical obstacles

|  | Average Number of Days Missed Due to Sickness[1] | Average Number of Days Missed Due to Logistical Obstacles[2] |
|---|---|---|
| White | 2.3 | 1.8 |
| Latino | 3.5 | 2.8 |
| African American | 3.9 | 4.1 |

**Note:** [1]This statistic is only calculated for preschool students who missed school because of sickness and it assumes that every student was enrolled for a total of 34 days during the teacher log data collection period. n=703. [2]This statistic is only calculated for preschool students who missed school because of a logistical obstacle and it assumes that every student was enrolled for a total of 34 days during the teacher log data collection period. n=318.

**Data Source:** Attendance logs.

students, and also white students, in the number of absences due to logistical challenges. African American students missed more days of school due to logistics (4 percent) than both white students (1 percent), and Latino students (1.5 percent; see Figure 12). During the nine-week log collection period, 38 percent of African American preschoolers missed at least a day of school because of transportation, child care, or family reasons, compared with only 16 percent of white students and 22 percent of Latino students (see Figure 13). Moreover, not only were there higher proportions of African American students missing school because of logistical challenges, but those who did encounter these struggles each missed more days of school (4.1 days on average) than white or Latino students who encountered similar struggles (1.8 and 2.8 days respectively; see Table 4).

## How Do Family, Parent, and School Factors Affect Attendance?

### Family factors play an important role in regular student attendance.

Absences are more prevalent in families where parents are single, are young, are in poor health, and rely on public transportation or emergency room care. The ways in which families manage sickness and logistical obstacles can make a difference in their children's preschool attendance.

Based on parent/guardian responses to a survey we administered and follow-up interviews conducted with

### FIGURE 13

Higher proportions of African American students missed school during a nine-week period because parents faced a logistical obstacle, compared to Latino and white students

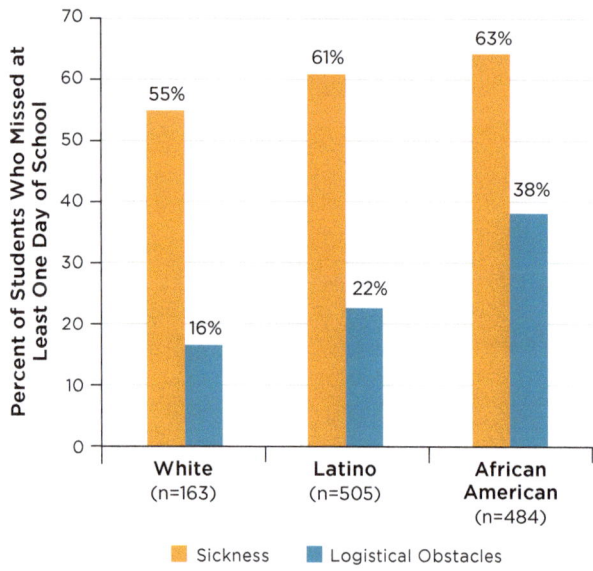

**Date Source:** Attendance logs; n=1,152

# How We Collected Data on Why Students Miss School

With the help and support of the Office of Early Childhood Education at CPS (OECE), UChicago CCSR collected data from several different sources during the 2011-12 school year to better understand reasons behind preschool absences. These included attendance logs, parent surveys, and parent interviews. We also collected survey responses from teachers to understand aspects of elementary school culture. Below we describe data collection efforts for each. **See Appendix A** for further details about data collection activities, a description of the samples, and specifics about data analysis.

## Attendance Logs

Teachers in a random stratified sample of 57 classrooms were asked to fill out logs in which they recorded reasons students were absent. Logs were filled out for a three-week period at three different points of the year (November, February, and April/May). Once a student returned to the classroom after being absent, teachers were asked to inquire about the reason for the absence from either the student or the parent/guardian. Teachers then indicated on the log form which of 14 possible categories corresponded most closely to the reason given. These categories were: doctor's visit (but not sick); sick (non-chronic); chronic illness; lack of transportation; caregiver arrangements; school phobia/separation anxiety; personal time/vacation; lack of sleep; family-related reason; violence/safety; weather; religion; other; do not know. There was additional space for the teacher to write notes if s/he could elaborate on the reason. These attendance logs provided data on 1,229 students; these students were highly representative of the full population of CPS preschool students.

## Parent Surveys

In the same sample of 57 classrooms in which teachers were asked to fill out attendance logs, CCSR and OECE staff conducted surveys of parents on report card pick-up day. The survey was available in both English and Spanish. Within these classrooms, over 90 percent of parents who came to school on report card pick-up day agreed to fill out a survey, giving us an overall response rate of 56 percent of all students in our sample of classrooms. The sample of students for whom we had parent survey responses was similar to the full CPS preschool population, except these students were more likely to be four years old and have lower absence rates (**see Tables A.1 and A.5 in Appendix A**).

## Parent Interviews

On the parent survey, we asked parents to indicate if they would be willing to participate in a follow-up interview about their answers to survey questions. Roughly 65 percent of parents agreed to be interviewed (n=376). We selected 40 families that represented a range of student attendance levels, and we conducted follow-up phone interviews with them. We administered the interviews in both English and Spanish. Overall, the children of these 40 parents were more likely to be African American and come from high-poverty neighborhoods than the overall CPS preschool population, but these children had similar average absence rates as the overall population. The interviews focused on parents' feelings about their child's preschool education, and parents' explanations of the reasons that cause their child to miss preschool. Interviews were conducted over the phone and lasted between 20 and 30 minutes.

## Teacher Survey Items

Each spring, the University of Chicago Urban Education Institute (UChicago UEI) administers a survey to all teachers across the CPS district. A number of questions were added to the 2012 survey specifically for preschool teachers. Teachers were also asked questions that have been included in the survey for many years about school climate and working conditions. **Table A.6 in Appendix A** displays the items used in our analyses and indicates whether the items were administered to all teachers in the school or only to preschool teachers.

a sub-sample of survey respondents, absence rates of preschool students differed significantly due to a number of family factors, many of which are associated with low socioeconomic status. For instance, children who were being raised by a single or widowed parent had higher absence rates, on average, than children who were being raised by adults who were married, divorced, or had a partner (see Figure 14). Several of the parents we interviewed expressed that having an extra adult within a family to help get a child to/from preschool allowed for better management of the logistics around school-going. One parent talked about sharing the responsibility for getting her daughter to and from school with her husband and other family members:

> If I [was] here at work, my husband would drop her off [at school]. And when I would get off of work, I would pick her up...And if I knew that [my husband] wasn't able to drop her off, I would be off or I would have [a family member] drop her off.

This may be particularly true when programs run only for half of the day, but is also the case with full-day programs that may not perfectly align with parents' own work or school schedules.

Family health circumstances were also related to student attendance. As **Figure 14** shows, students who received their primary medical care from emergency rooms missed more days of school than children who received primary medical care from a private doctor, a clinic, or another type of medical facility. Similarly, parents with poorer health had children who missed more school than parents with better health. Because preschool students rely on their parents to get them to school, parental illness can make transportation difficult.

Logistical challenges may be harder when parents do not drive or walk their children to school. Children whose families relied on public transportation to get to school had worse attendance than children who drove or walked (see Figure 14). Public transportation not only tends to take longer than personal transportation but also is subject to such problems as late buses, missed buses, and overcrowding.

**FIGURE 14**

Children who are in single-parent families, live in high-poverty neighborhoods, have parents with fair or poor health, or take public transportation have higher absence rates than peers without these circumstances

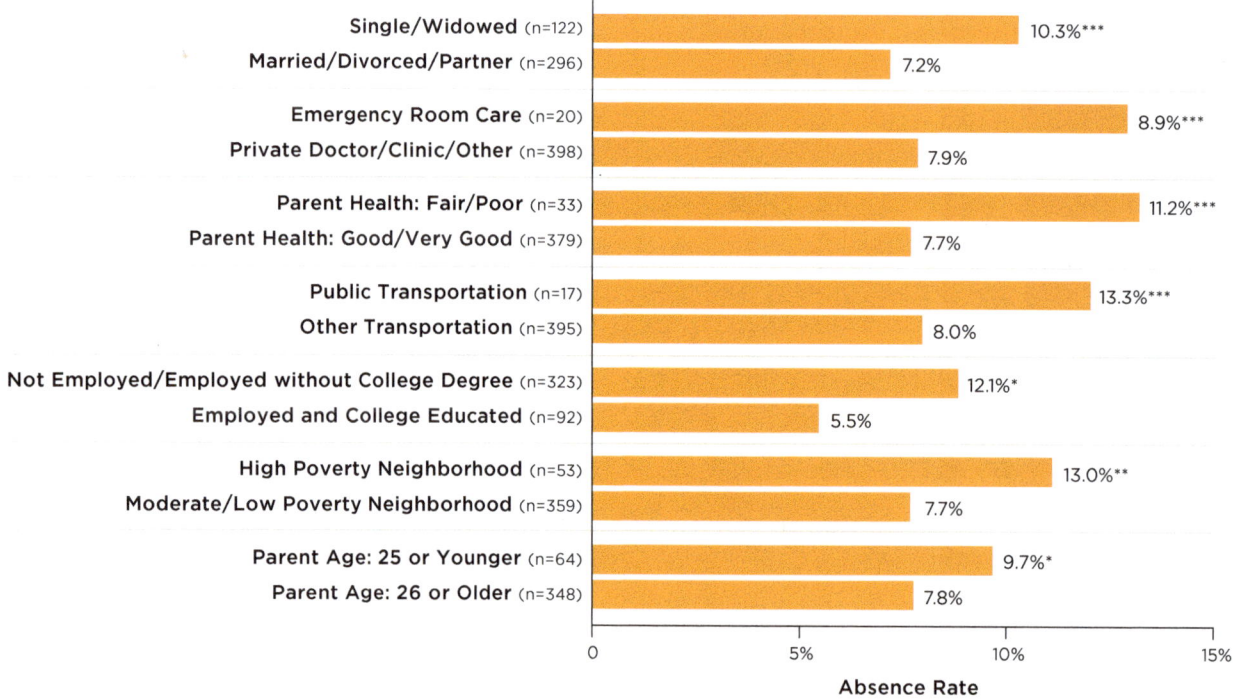

**Data Source:** Parent Survey, absence rate over 2011-12 school year
**Note:** *Indicates that absence rates are significantly different from those of the comparison category: p<.05 level, **p<.01, ***p<.001

Other factors associated with income, poverty, and education were related to attendance. Children whose parents were college educated and employed had better attendance than other children. Similarly, children who lived in low- or moderate-poverty neighborhoods attended school more regularly than children living in high-poverty neighborhoods. Finally, children whose parents were 25 years old or younger missed more days of school than children with older parents.

Many families in our sample experienced more than one of these challenging family circumstances. The more circumstances they faced, the worse their child's attendance was (**see Figure 15**). Children in families that did not face any of these circumstances had an absence rate of 5.6 percent, on average; those facing one circumstance had an absence rate of 7.5 percent; and those facing two circumstances had an absence rate of 9 percent, on average. Children whose families were faced with three or more challenging circumstances missed nearly 13 percent of total enrolled days, meaning they were chronically absent.

**FIGURE 15**

**The more challenging circumstances a family faces, the higher preschool students absence rates are**

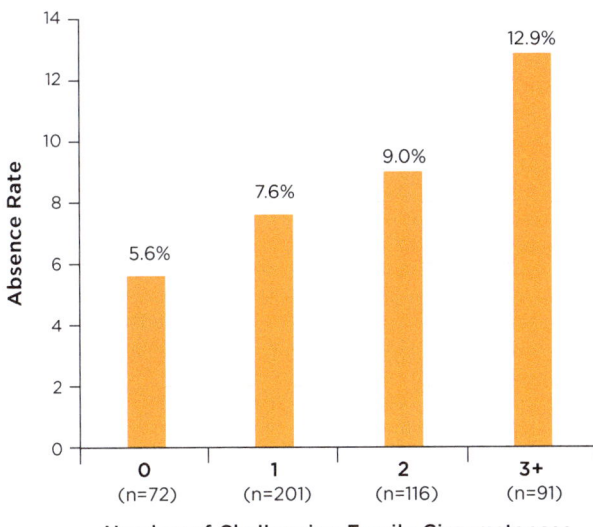

**Data Source:** Parent survey, absence rate over 2011-12 school year; n=480.

**Note:** Challenging family circumstances include having a single/widowed parent, having a parent who is either unemployed or employed without a college degree, living in a high-poverty neighborhood, having a parent with fair/poor health, relying on public transportation to get to/from school, relying on the emergency room for primary medical care, and having a parent who is 25 years old or younger.

We know that families tend to experience more than one challenging circumstance; thus, it is important to determine which of these circumstances is independently related to absenteeism and which is related to absenteeism only because it is related to another factor (e.g., relying on emergency medical care might be related to attendance independently or, alternatively, might simply be a marker of poverty, which also is related to attendance). To consider this question, we used a multivariate analysis to determine which of these were significantly related to preschool students' absence rates, even after controlling for all the other circumstances. We found that most of the challenging family circumstances described above remained significantly related to students' attendance, meaning that they were uniquely related to attendance, even after controlling for all other circumstances simultaneously. Parents' marital status, parental education and employment, parental health, and source of primary medical care were all significantly associated with preschool students' absence rates; only neighborhood poverty level, parental age, and use of public transportation to get to school were no longer significantly associated with preschool students' absence rates once we considered other challenging circumstances. The fact that neighborhood poverty level was not significantly related to students' attendance after controlling for other circumstances suggests that neighborhood resources—whether financial or social—work through these other family circumstances. Being college educated and having a job may provide families with more of these resources. Parents with more financial resources may have greater access to quality medical care, which in turn may be related to better overall health and ultimately better attendance. Financial and social resources may also be important for managing logistical challenges that arise due to child care, transportation, and other family-related issues. For a look at how these factors contribute to the racial gap in attendance, see *Explaining the Race Gap in Attendance* on p.32.

# Explaining the Race Gap in Attendance

Many of the family circumstances associated with lower preschool attendance are disproportionately experienced by African American families and, in some cases, Latino families, which contributes to their children's higher absence rates compared to white children. For example, only 15 percent of African American children and 11 percent of Latino children in our sample had a parent or guardian who was employed and had a college degree, compared to one-third of all white preschool students (**see Figure 16**). More than half of all African American preschool students in our sample lived with a single parent (59 percent) compared to only 7 percent of white preschool students and 16 percent of Latino students (**see Figure 17**). Around 10 percent of African American and Latino preschool students had a parent with poor or fair health compared to only 1 percent of white preschool students (**see Figure 18**). While only 10 percent of African American preschool students relied on public transportation to get to school and nine percent relied on emergency rooms for primary care, they were far more likely to rely on these services than either white or Latino students (**see Figures 19 and 20**). Among all of these family circumstances, the ones that were most strongly associated with higher absence rates among African American preschool students compared to white students were differences in marital status and parent education and employment (**see Appendix A** for more details of this analysis). However, differences in parent health, transportation, and medical care were also associated with higher absence rates for African American preschool students compared to white students. For Latino students, lower levels of parental education and employment were the factors most strongly associated with higher absence rates, compared to white students.

### FIGURE 16
**Parents' education and employment status by race**

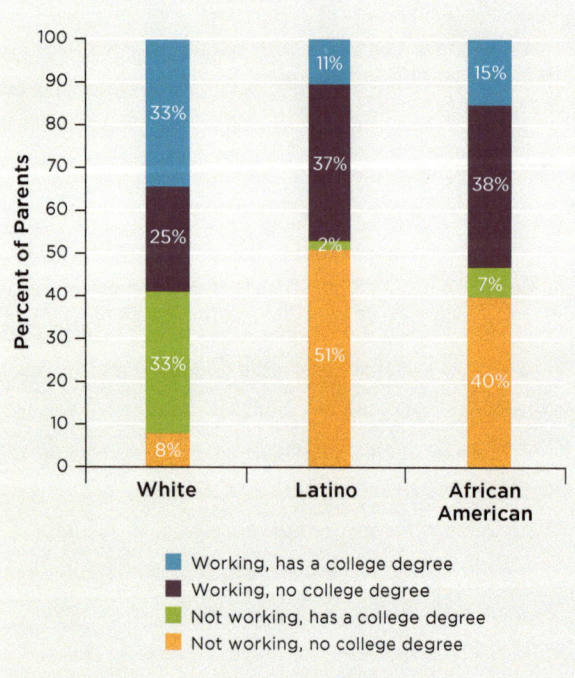

### FIGURE 17
**Parents' marital status by race**

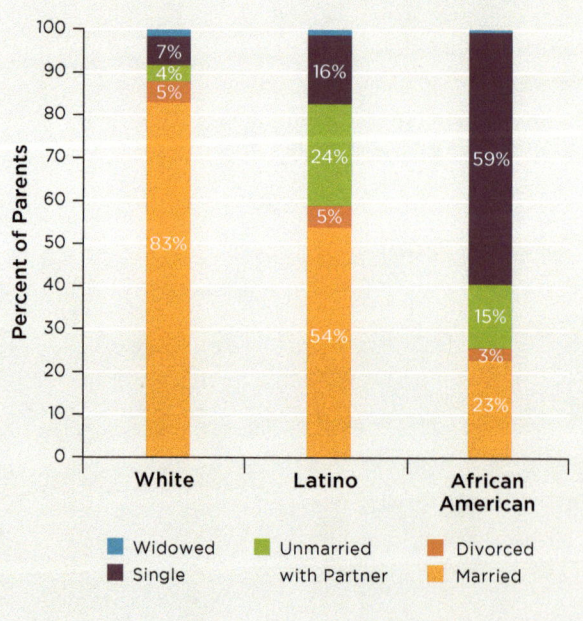

Date Source: Parent survey; n=451.

# EXPLAINING THE RACE GAP... *CONTINUED*

**FIGURE 18**
Quality of parent health by race

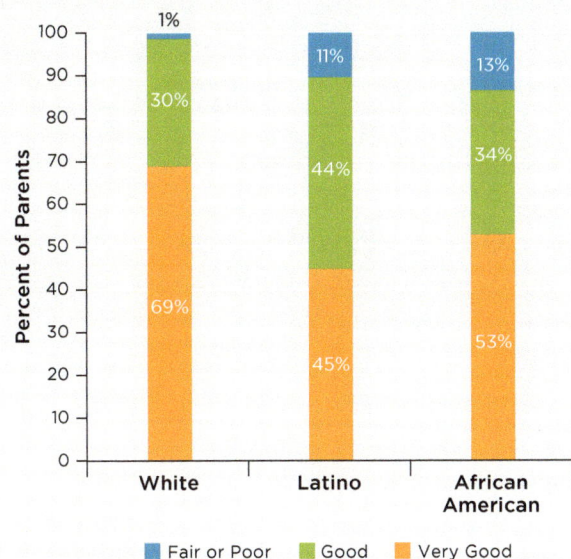

**Date Source:** Parent survey; n=449.

**FIGURE 19**
Transportation to school by race

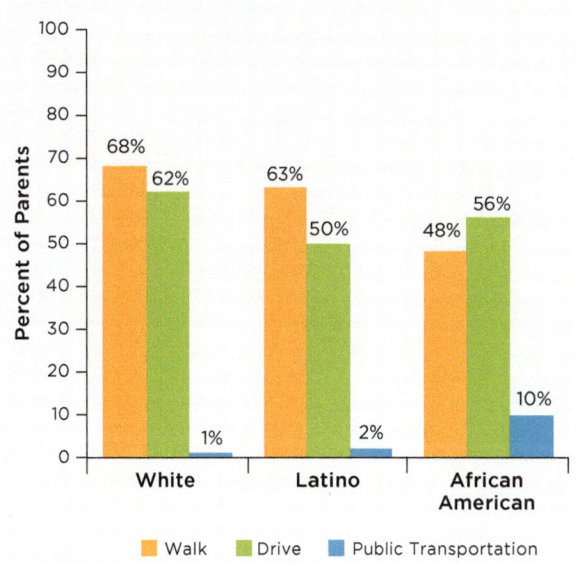

**Date Source:** Parent survey; n=448.

**FIGURE 20**
Source of primary medical care by race

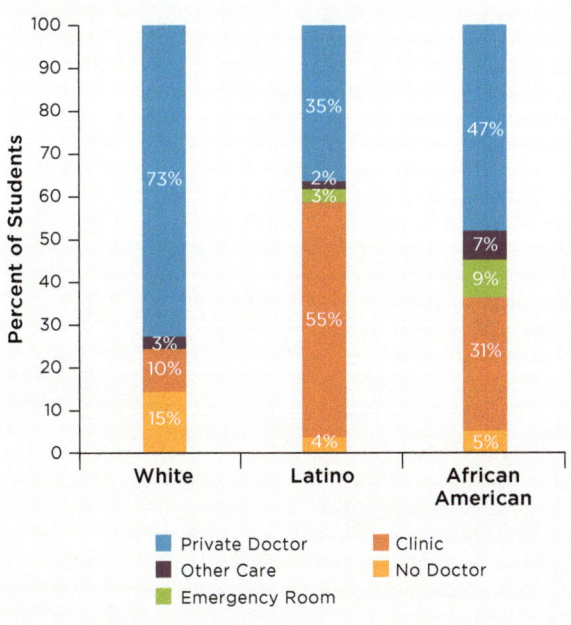

**Date Source:** Parent survey; n=403.

Chapter 3 | Reasons for Preschool Absences

**Parental beliefs about attendance are important.**
While family circumstances matter for how often children attend preschool, so do parent beliefs about the importance of regular attendance during preschool. Parents with stronger beliefs about the importance of regular attendance in preschool had children with better attendance. Most parents believed that attendance was important, but those who thought attendance mattered less in the preschool years than in the older grades had children who missed preschool more often.

Most parents we interviewed (26 out of 39) expressed that it was important their children attend preschool every day. Some held a general belief that education was important; others did not want their child to miss out on learning and/or fall behind by missing school. However, within these groups of parents, there was a distinction between those who felt attendance was just as important as it would be when their child was older (such as in third grade) and those who did not. Those who believed that attendance in the earliest years was as important as later on (n=13) explained that instilling regular school attendance during the preschool years sets the stage for good attendance later on and is an important part of the foundation of learning. One parent said,

> We try not to [miss school]...I'm very much in the mindset of they go to school every day, just because that instills the importance of school in them more so than that they're gonna miss any particular lesson that day. You know, I don't think it's gonna be hard to [catch up if they miss], but I think instilling that importance and the priorities of going to school on a regular basis [matters].

Other parents felt that, although it is important in preschool, attendance would be more important in later years (n=12). These parents explained that it is easier to fall behind as their child gets older. One parent said, *"[It's going to matter more later since] there's more to learn, and there's more to miss out on, so if he don't make it, you know, in third grade, if you miss a day, you miss a lot."*

The remaining parents we interviewed said that preschool attendance was either "somewhat" important to them (7 out of 39) or not very important (7 out of 39).

Some said that, while they would like for their child to attend school when possible, sometimes various things *"happen"* that result in a missed day of school—such as illness, family vacation, or other family emergencies. One parent said, *"I'd prefer her not to miss. If she's sick, she's sick...I think I also feel like if there's some big thing going on or an opportunity I can take her to—like, we travel quite a bit—I would pull her out for that."*

In general, these parents believed that their child would be learning more at older ages, and it would be harder to catch up if s/he missed a day of school. They expressed that while their child was in preschool it was easy for him/her to catch up on what s/he missed because their child's preschool program was *"only two-and-a-half hours"* long; there was no curriculum, and preschool was all play; and/or their child was learning what s/he needed to at home. One parent stated,

> It really don't [matter when Ebony misses a day of school] 'cause she's learning the same things I've already taught her...So, when she's at home I'm teaching her, too...The reason why I put her in school is because she does need to interact with other kids...I thought she was gonna learn something I wasn't gonna teach her, but it's the same thing that I teach her, so...in preschool, it's like all they are doing is playing.

**FIGURE 21**

**Parental beliefs about the importance of regular preschool attendance are related to children's attendance**

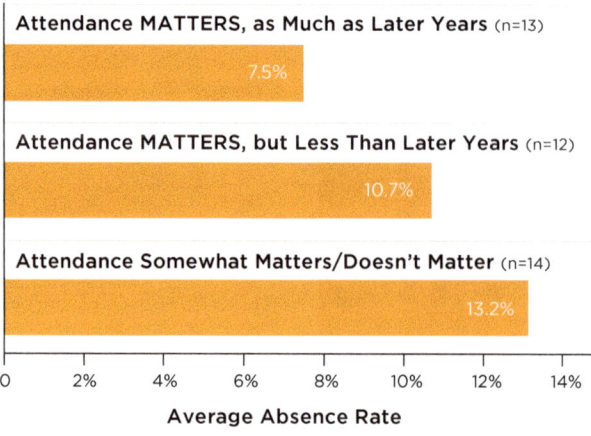

**Data Source:** Parent interview; n=39.

Figure 21 shows that children whose parents believe preschool attendance is as important as in later years had the lowest absence rates (an average of 7.5 percent). In comparison, children whose parents said that preschool attendance was important but would be even more important in later years had absence rates of 10.7 percent, on average. Finally, children whose parents did not believe that regular attendance in preschool matters much had the highest absence rates, with an average of 13.2 percent.[31]

### Attendance is better in safe, orderly schools.

As we showed in the previous section, parents' attitudes about the importance of preschool attendance are related to their children's attendance rates. This suggests that children may attend more when there is a strong connection between families and schools. One key factor in building this strong connection is having a positive school climate—including high levels of teacher-parent trust and parent involvement within the school. Other factors may also be important. For example, Bryk and colleagues (2010) found that a school's level of safety and orderliness was the school factor most strongly associated with whether an elementary school showed improvement in student attendance over a seven-year period. In addition, schools with a strong instructional program and schools in which there was a strong professional commitment among teachers were also more likely to show improvement in attendance compared to schools that were weak on these dimensions.

Using teacher survey responses from the 2012 survey, we examined whether these same school climate measures—including teacher-parent trust, parent involvement in the school, school safety, and teachers' commitment to their school—were related to preschools' average attendance rates.[32] We also examined whether preschool teachers' feelings of connectedness to the rest of their elementary school were related to their preschool students' attendance.[33] Finally, we looked at whether a classroom's instructional supports, as measured by the Classroom Assessment Scoring System (CLASS),[34] were related to the average attendance of students in that classroom.[35]

Schools that enroll similar student populations have different average absence rates that vary with the school climate. Consistent with earlier research, the climate factor most strongly associated with average absence was the level of safety reported by teachers at the school; preschool students were absent less often in schools in which teachers reported feeling safe (**see Table 5**). Although very few preschool parents who responded to our survey listed safety as a top reason why their child missed school, it may be the case that an unsafe school environment helps to foster an overall indifference about the importance of regular attendance. In addition, preschool students missed fewer days when they attended schools in which trust between parents and teachers was strong, parent involvement was high, and teachers felt a strong commitment to their school. Absences were also lower in schools where preschool teachers reported feeling more connected to the elementary school as whole. While we do not have a clear understanding of why this connection matters for attendance, we speculate that in these schools there is a more explicit and shared recognition of the importance of preschool for preparing students for kindergarten and beyond, which may be felt not only by teachers but also by parents. When schools are strong on safety, parent involvement, trust, teacher commitment, or preschool teacher inclusion, their preschool students have an overall absence rate that is one-and-a-half percentage points lower than schools that are weak on the same component, after taking into account the background characteristics of students enrolled in the school.

**TABLE 5**

**Correlations between average adjusted attendance rates and school/classroom climate measures**

| School and Classroom Climate Measures | Correlation with Adjusted Preschool Absence Rate |
|---|---|
| Teacher-Parent Trust[1] | -0.21*** |
| Parent Involvement[1] | -0.20*** |
| School Safety[1] | -0.26*** |
| Preschool Inclusion[1] | -0.20*** |
| School Commitment[1] | -0.19*** |
| Classroom Instructional Supports[2] | -0.12* |

**Notes:** Adjusted preschool absence rates take into account students' race, gender, ELL status, special education status, neighborhood poverty level, and socioeconomic status, and the distance traveled to school. (1) Indicates a school level measure; n=341. (2) Indicates a classroom level measure; n=288.

A classroom's instructional quality was also significantly related to preschool attendance: students missed fewer days of school when the instructional quality of their classroom was high; however, the relationship between absences and classroom instructional quality was not as strong as the relationships with other climate factors. On average, absence rates were about half a point lower in classrooms where instructional quality was high compared to classrooms where instructional quality was low. As our findings in this chapter have shown, families play an important role in whether their children attend preschool regularly. The aspects of school life that parents experience most directly, such as relationships with school staff and school safety, seem to matter more for children's attendance than the quality of the instructional program.

## Summary

Many preschool students miss school because they are sick. In fact, illness accounted for just over half of all days missed during a nine-week period. However, African American and Latino students missed twice as many days of school due to sickness than white students. African American students were also far more likely to miss school because their parents struggled with an array of logistical challenges in getting their children to school, including transportation, child care issues, and family-related issues. Challenging family circumstances — unemployment and low levels of parent education, single family households, poor health among family members, and reliance on emergency rooms or medical care — may make it harder for families to manage sickness and logistical obstacles.

Other factors may play a role in whether children attend preschool regularly. Parents who believe their children's school attendance is as important in preschool as in later grades have children who begin their educational career with better attendance than other children. But parents are not alone in being able to make a difference; there is evidence suggesting schools can contribute to setting a culture that supports better attendance. School organization may play a role in fostering good attendance, and school leaders can create structures that support family efforts to get their students to school every day. In the next chapter, we discuss the implications of these findings and others for understanding and addressing chronic absenteeism.

CHAPTER 4

# Interpretive Summary

Chronic absenteeism is common among CPS preschool students and has significant implications for these students' kindergarten readiness and future attendance patterns, which may have a detrimental effect on their learning outcomes in later grades. Schools' ability to organize themselves to support preschool attendance may be key to preventing later problems.

Chronic absenteeism in preschool is a significant problem, with more than one-third of all four-year-old CPS preschool students missing 10 percent or more of school. Chronically absent preschool students not only have lower levels of academic and social-emotional kindergarten readiness, but they also are more likely to be chronically absent in subsequent grades. Among students with multiple years of chronic absenteeism between preschool and second grade, many need intervention in order to be reading at grade level by third grade. The link between preschool attendance and learning outcomes highlights a need to understand and address the roots of chronic absenteeism among preschool students. Doing so may ensure that more students are prepared for kindergarten. It may also help to turn around problematic patterns at the very earliest stage of a student's educational career, before a cumulative toll has occurred from irregular attendance over multiple years.

As schools consider what they can do to improve preschool students' attendance, they may feel that many of the factors contributing to high rates of absenteeism are beyond their control. Typical childhood illnesses (e.g., colds, flu, and stomach viruses) account for more than half of all school days missed. Other factors (e.g., transportation, child care issues, and poor family health), which contribute disproportionately to poor attendance among African American students, may seem even more intractable since they are deeply connected with societal problems like poverty and lack of access to quality health care. Yet, schools may be able to make a difference. Schools serving similar populations of students do have different attendance rates, which is related to the climate, and presumably on the policies and practices of the school.

Improving attendance within a school may require a multi-tiered approach, much like the Response to Intervention (RtI) approach.[36] This could involve implementing broad, school-wide approaches to monitoring and supporting attendance; more targeted approaches for students who are at risk of chronic absenteeism; and intensive interventions for chronically absent students. The specific approaches, and the focus on each level of intervention, will vary across schools.

At the school-wide level, collecting and monitoring data on all students' attendance is an important first step. For students whose attendance falls within a warning level, schools may create plans for reaching out to parents to help them understand the importance of preschool and strategize on how to improve attendance. Schools may also consider partnering with local organizations to help remove some of the barriers to regular attendance. In the next sections, we extrapolate on these strategies that may contribute to better attendance.

## Collecting, Monitoring Data is an Important Step for Improving Attendance

Illinois is one of only a few states that do not require schools to report student attendance, which may mean there is very little incentive for districts or schools to collect and monitor how often students are absent from school. Even in states that do require attendance data to be reported, schools and districts are typically held accountable for average daily attendance, which, as we describe in Chapter 1, can mask larger attendance problems. A better indicator of potential attendance issues at the school level is the percent of students in a school who are chronically absent. By tracking chronic absence rates at schools, districts can determine the degree to which schools may need support and strategies for getting more students to come to school regularly.

Identifying individual students who are chronically absent is also important for addressing attendance issues within a school. Monthly or biweekly watch lists that highlight those students who miss more than a particular number of days may prove useful, so that teachers can reach out to parents to help develop strategies for attending more regularly.[37, 38] Sharing preschool attendance records with kindergarten teachers as students transition to the next grade level may help elementary schools maintain a sustained and consistent approach to improving attendance over time. Kindergarten teachers might reach out to families of students who were chronically absent in preschool early, as soon as they start to miss school. Breaking the cycle of multiple years of chronic absenteeism early on may be a critical step toward improving the learning trajectories of students with the highest risk of chronic absenteeism.

## Communicating with Families May Help Improve Attendance

As schools strategize on how to best support improved attendance, the greatest chances of success will happen when a working relationship exists between schools and families. While many of the factors that are related to preschool attendance are struggles that families face outside the school building, schools may be able to improve student attendance by working together with families. In fact, outreach and relationship building with parents is often intended to be a key component of preschool programs, such as Head Start, where one goal of the program is to have *"parents and families observe, guide, promote, and participate in the everyday learning of their children at home, school, and in their communities."*[39] As parents become directly involved in their child's learning and have stronger relationships with their child's teacher, there is a greater support for academic advancement.[40] And these efforts to increase communication and make connections between schools and parents are related to improvements in student attendance.[41]

There is value in messaging the importance of preschool attendance to parents. While most parents we interviewed said that regular attendance in preschool is important, not all parents believed it was as important as regular attendance in the elementary grades; these beliefs were then related to their children's attendance in preschool. Because parent attitudes do play a role in whether children come to school regularly, providing parents with information on the ways in which preschool attendance matters for their child's learning and educational trajectory may encourage them to focus on attendance with their own child. By showing the relationship between attendance in preschool and kindergarten readiness, schools can point to compelling evidence that regular attendance may be important for preparing young children for kindergarten, both academically and socially.

More targeted efforts may be necessary for students who enter preschool with low levels of incoming skills. These students are the most likely to miss a large amount of preschool, and they benefit the most from regular attendance. It may help to develop a partnership before problems occur by reaching out to these parents at the beginning of the school year, before the student is frequently absent, to develop strategies for students' learning that include regular attendance. Forging trust between parents and teachers around issues of attendance is critical. In doing so, it is important that parents not feel they are being blamed for their child's high rates of absenteeism but instead feel that they are being engaged in a process of figuring out how to provide their child with the best learning opportunities by getting them to school more regularly. Teachers can use data on the relationship between attendance and later outcomes to show concern about the student's future and keep conversations focused on what to do to help the child gain as much as possible from his/her preschool experience.

Families and communities differ in the particular needs and challenges they face in making sure their children attend preschool regularly. Thus improving attendance of very young children is likely to require a *"student by student, family by family"* approach. The pre-existing emphasis on family involvement in preschool provides an opportunity for teachers to build relationships with parents of chronically absent students to understand the specific reasons why some students miss so much school and develop strategies among members of the school community to address common issues.

## Partnering with Local Organizations May Help Schools Improve Attendance

As we have seen, absences do not occur in a vacuum; they are attached to a range of difficulties that families face. While schools cannot reasonably be expected to solve many of the issues that lead to very high rates of absenteeism (e.g., poor family health, child care, and transportation), they may be able to partner with community organizations that can assist with some of these challenges or figure out ways to help families to support each other (e.g., through carpools and information sharing). Community partnerships may prove particularly useful in two areas that substantially contribute to preschool absences—poor student and family health, and the half-day preschool schedule.

- **Poor student and family health.** Missing many days of school because of sickness and poor parental health is a significant issue for some preschool children, especially African American students. Schools in which sick rates are especially high might consider establishing close relationships with community health organizations that can provide health services to families. For example, partnerships with health organizations could teach parents about how to manage young children's sickness, particularly asthma.[42] Health organizations may also be able to provide important health screening, diagnostics, or health care for children and their families. Finally, community health partnerships may be able to provide parents with important information about medical care resources available in their community, so that families do not need to rely on emergency rooms for medical care.

- **The half-day schedule.** The half-day schedule provided by most CPS preschools creates a logistical challenge for many parents. Half-day programs have become increasingly prevalent, especially with the rise in numbers of three- and four-year-olds being served alongside simultaneous decreases in funding.[43] But parents described that having school for only two-and-a-half or three hours a day was difficult to plan around. While lengthening the school day is not likely given current fiscal constraints, supplementing the existing half-day programs with other community-based learning opportunities may increase children's learning in several ways. First, it could increase exposure to educational programming, and thus time on task. Being in a learning environment for a longer period of time—particularly for children who are not likely to be developing kindergarten-readiness skills at home—expands the opportunities children have to learn. Second, it may increase overall attendance of young children. If half-day programming deters parents from getting their children to school every day, maybe full-day programming (or supplemental programming of some sort) will make it easier for children to come to school every day. It might also send a message to parents that missing a day of school can undermine their child's development towards readiness for kindergarten.

There are other ways community partnerships may also promote better attendance. For instance, some neighborhood organizations utilize parents to reach out to other parents, helping to create social networks for families. Schools that partner with community-based organizations may jointly be able to figure out additional strategies to address the schools', families', and students' particular challenges, while engaging families in the process, and thus building trust.

## Conclusion

Poor school attendance, beginning in the earliest of years, is one of the first indicators that a child may be struggling—both at home and at school. Indeed, for some children early absenteeism is just the beginning of many years of missing substantial amounts of school. But attendance can also be thought of as a powerful lever. Focusing on preschool children with poor attendance and reaching out to families to address obstacles provides schools and early education programs with the earliest opportunity to engage families and change the course of a student's educational trajectory.

At the local and national level, policymakers have been aiming to provide more and more children with access to a high quality preschool education. However, the quality of that education is not only tied to the emotional and instructional supports available for children and families in early education programs. It also relies on the assumption that children are regularly attending school. That means that just enrolling children in preschool is not enough. Ensuring that preschool students attend regularly is a critical component in preparing them for kindergarten and beyond, particularly for students who have low levels of prior skills. Schools may not be able solve all of the issues that keep students from coming to school, but they can work on strategies to get students to school despite those issues. Focusing on and improving attendance has the potential to redirect struggling children onto the pathway towards educational success.

# References

Allensworth, E.M., and Easton, J.Q. (2007)
*What matters for staying on-track and graduating in Chicago Public Schools: A close look at course grades, failures, and attendance in the freshman year.* Chicago, IL: University of Chicago Consortium on Chicago School Research.

Annie E. Casey Foundation. (2010)
*Early warning: Why reading by the end of third grade matters.* Baltimore, MD: Author.

Balfanz, R., and Byrnes, V. (2012)
*The importance of being in school: A report on absenteeism in the nation's public schools.* Baltimore: Johns Hopkins University Center for Social Organization of Schools.

Barnett, W.S., Carolan, M.E., Fitzgerald, J., and Squires, J.H. (2011)
*The state of preschool 2001. State preschool yearbook.* New Brunswick, NJ: The National Institute for Early Education Research.

Bitler, M.P., Hoynes, H.W., and Domina, T. (2013)
Experimental evidence on distributional effects of Head Start. Retrieved August 7, 2013, from http://www.socsci.uci.edu/%7Embitler/papers/bdh-hsis-paper.pdf.

Bloom B., Cohen, R.A., Freeman, G. (2012)
Summary Health Statistics for U.S. Children: National Health Interview Survey, 20011. National Center for Health Statistics. *Vital Health Stat 10*(254).

Bloom B., Dey, A.N., Freeman, G. (2006)
Summary Health Statistics for U.S. Children: National Health Interview Survey, 2005. National Center for Health Statistics. *Vital Health Stat 10*(231).

Bryk, A.S., Sebring, P.B., Allensworth, E., Luppescu, S., and Easton, J.Q. (2010)
*Organizing schools for improvement: Lessons from Chicago.* Chicago, IL: The University of Chicago Press.

Burchinal, M., Peisner-Feinberg, E., Pianta, R.C., and Howes, C. (2002)
Development of academic skills from preschool through second grade: Family and classroom predictors of developmental trajectories. *Journal of School Psychology, 40,* 415-436.

Campbell, F.A., Pungello, E.P., Miller-Johnson, S., Burchinal, M., and Ramey, C.T. (2001)
The development of cognitive and academic abilities: Growth curves from an early childhood educational experiment. *Developmental Psychology, 37,* 231-242.

Case, A., Lubotsky, D., and Paxson, C. (2002)
Economic status and health in childhood: The origins of the gradient. *The American Economic Review, 92,* 1308-1334.

Chang, H.N., and Romero, M. (2008)
*Present, engaged and accounted for: The critical importance of addressing chronic absence in the early grades.* New York, NY: National Center for Children in Poverty (NCCP): The Mailman School of Public Health at Columbia University.

Chicago Public Schools (2012)
*At a Glance.* Chicago, IL: Chicago Public Schools Office of Early Childhood Education.

Connolly, F., and Olsen, L.S. (2012)
*Early elementary performance and attendance in Baltimore City Schools' pre-kindergarten and kindergarten.* Baltimore, MD: Baltimore Education Research Consortium.

Good, R.H., and Kaminski, R.A. (2002)
*Dynamic Indicators of Basic Early Literacy Skills (6th ed.).* Eugene, OR: Institute for the Development of Educational Achievement.

Good, R.H., Wallin, J., Simmons, D.C., Kame'enui, E.J., and Kaminski, R.A. (2002)
*System-wide Percentile Ranks for DIBELS Benchmark Assessment (Technical Report 9).* Eugene, OR: University of Oregon.

Heckman, J.J. (2011)
The economics of inequality. The value of early childhood education. *American Educator, 35,* 31-35, 47.

Jaffe, L.E. (2009)
*Development, interpretation, and application of the W score and the relative proficiency index* (Woodcock-Johnson III Assessment Service Bulletin No. 11). Rolling Meadows, IL: Riverside Publishing.

Kearney, C.A., and Graczyk, P. (2013)
A Response to Intervention model to promote school attendance and decrease school absenteeism. *Child Youth Care Forum*, published online. doi: 10.1007/s10566-013-9222-1.

Neild, R.C., Balfanz, R., and Herzog, L. (2007)
Early intervention at every age. *Educational Leadership, 65,* 28-33.

Pianta, R.C., La Paro, K.M., and Hamre, B.K. (2007)
*Classroom Assessment Scoring System (CLASS).* Baltimore, MD: Paul H. Brookes Publishing Co.

Plank, S., Durham, R.E., Farley-Ripple, E., and Norman, O. (June 2008)
*First grade and forward: A seven year examination within the Baltimore City Public School System.* Baltimore: Baltimore Education Research Consortium.

Ramey, C.T., and Ramey, S.L. (1998)
Early intervention and early experience. *American Psychologist, 53,* 109-120.

Ready, D.D. (2010)
Socioeconomic disadvantage, school attendance, and early cognitive development: The differential effects of school exposure. *Sociology of Education, 83,* 271-286.

Reynolds, A.J. Temple, J.A., Ou, S., Robertson, D. L., Mersky, J.P., Topitzes, J.W. and Niles, M.D. (2007)
Effects of a school-based, early childhood intervention on adult health and well-being: A 19-year follow-up of low-income families. *Archives of Pediatrics & Adolescent Medicine, 161,* 730-739.

Romero, M., and Lee, Y. (2007)
*A national portrait of chronic absenteeism in the early grades.* New York: National Center for Children in Poverty, Columbia University.

Rush, K.L. (1999)
Caregiver-child interactions and early literacy development of preschool children from low-income environments. *Topics in Early Childhood Special Education, 19,* 3-14.

Schweinhart, L.J., Montie, J., Xiang, Z., Barnett, W.S., Belfield, C.R., and Nores, M. (2005)
*Lifetime effects: The HighScope Perry Preschool study through age 40* (Monographs of the HighScope Educational Research Foundation, 14). Ypsilanti, MI: HighScope Press.

Sheldon, S.B. (2007)
Improving student attendance with school, family, and community partnerships. *The Journal of Educational Research, 100,* 267-275.

Sheldon, S.B., and Epstein, J.L. (2004)
Getting students to school: Using family and community involvement to reduce chronic absenteeism. *The School Community Journal, 14,* 39-56.

U.S. Department of Health and Human Services, Office of Head Start. (2011)
*The Head Start parent, family, and community engagement framework. Promoting family engagement and school readiness, from prenatal to age 8.* Washington, DC: U.S. Department of Health and Human Services, Administration for Children and Families, Office of Head Start.

Woodcock, R.W., McGrew, K.S., and Mather, N. (2001)
*Woodcock-Johnson III.* Rolling Meadows, IL: Riverside Publishing.

Woods, E.R., Bhaumik, U., Sommer, S.J., Ziniel, S.I., Kessler, A.J., Chan, E., and Nethersole, S. (2012)
Community Asthma Initiative: Evaluation of a quality improvement program for comprehensive asthma care. *Pediatrics, 129,* 465-472.

Wright, B. D., & Masters, G. N. (1982)
*Rating scale analysis: Rasch measurement.* Chicago, IL: MESA Press.

# Appendix A
## Data Sources, Description of Samples, and Analytic Methods

**Administrative data on student background and yearly attendance.** Administrative data on all Chicago Public School (CPS) students are collected by the district and shared with the University of Chicago Consortium on Chicago School Research (UChicago CCSR) twice a year. These data include student background information, such as gender, grade level, birthdate, free or reduced-price lunch eligibility, special education status, and home address. UChicago CCSR also receives end-of-year attendance data on all students, which provide the overall number of days each student is enrolled and absent each year. These records are available for all students in CPS.

**Data on neighborhood economic conditions.** Using the home address of each student, CCSR merges in census information about the neighborhood in which each student lives to create two measures of the economic conditions of students' residential block group. There are CPS students in 2,450 census block groups in the city; each block group is equivalent to about one city block. A measure of **neighborhood concentration of poverty** is constructed from data on the percent of adult males employed, and the percent of families with incomes above the poverty line. A measure of **neighborhood social status** is constructed from data on the mean level of education of adults and the percentage of employed persons who work as managers or professionals. Both neighborhood measures are standardized such that a 0 value is the mean value for census block groups in Chicago and 1 is the standard deviation. Half of the block groups will have a negative value, and half will have a positive value. Neighborhoods with a concentration of poverty value greater than 1 are considered high-poverty neighborhoods, those with values between -1 and 1 are considered moderate-poverty neighborhoods, and those with values below -1 are considered low-poverty neighborhoods. The concentration of poverty variable is especially useful for determining the poorest of the poor neighborhoods in the city because it is much more sensitive to differences than only using the simple free or reduced-price lunch variable.

**Data on daily attendance and program type.** For preschool attendance rates, the CPS Office of Early Childhood Education (OECE) provided attendance files for all three- and four-year-old CPS preschool students for the school years 2008-09 through 2011-12. These files allowed us to compare attendance rates across the year, and the duration and timing of periods of absence for each student. These files also provided ELL status for preschool students in 2010-11 and 2011-12. For our analyses, we excluded preschool students who were enrolled in a Montessori program or in a program specifically focused on children with special needs, in line with studies conducted by CPS.

**Cleaning daily attendance data files, 2008-09 through 2011-12:** CCSR worked closely with OECE to clean that data appropriately. First, we eliminated any students in the files who were never present over the school year. Second, and perhaps most importantly, we adjusted the data so that professional development (PD) days for teachers were not counted against students. During these school years, many preschool teachers had a half-day of professional development every Friday. This affected their morning sessions for about half of the year and their afternoon sessions for the other half of the year. On these days, students were marked as absent even though it was a non-enrollment day for them. Because PD days for teachers were not on a consistent calendar across all teachers, we adjusted days when nearly all students in a class were marked as having an excused absence and counted those as non-enrollment days. After this adjustment was made, the modal number of enrollment days for preschool students was around 150 days.

## Datasets for Examining Absenteeism in Preschool and the Early Grades

Using our adjusted daily preschool attendance files, student master files from CPS, and average yearly attendance for students in grades kindergarten and above, we created annual datasets for 2008-09 through 2011-12. For cross-sectional analyses on average absence rates and the percent of students chronically absent, we included students if they were either (1) in our preschool daily attendance files, were three or four years old, and listed as in preschool in our master file; or (2) were in our master file, were between the ages of five and eight, and in kindergarten through third grade (for the analysis of later grades). **Table A.1** displays the background characteristics of the preschool children included in our sample; **Table A.2** provides overall sample sizes for students ages five through eight included in cross-sectional analyses of absence rates. For three-year-olds enrolled in preschool in 2008-09, we also created a longitudinal dataset that contained records across all of the years, linked by student ID, to see how students' absences changed over time as they moved from preschool through third grade, following the same students across years.

Using the annual datasets, we first calculated average absence rates and the percent of students chronically absent for each age group of students in each year. Using the longitudinal dataset, we calculated average absence rates for the same students at ages three, four, five, and six.

To determine which background characteristics were most strongly associated with chronic absenteeism, we compared pseudo-R2 statistics from a series of logistic regressions in which chronic absenteeism was modeled as a function of each background characteristic individually and in combination. Background characteristics included race, gender, neighborhood poverty, neighborhood social status, special education status, and ELL status. Although we present neighborhood poverty categorically in **Figure 5, p.13**, it was analyzed as a continuous variable. Even with neighborhood poverty as a continuous variable, race was much more predictive of absence rates than neighborhood poverty.

### TABLE A.2
Sample size of cross-sectional analysis of absenteeism from ages five through eight

| Age | 2008-09 | 2009-10 | 2010-11 | 2011-12 |
|---|---|---|---|---|
| 5 | 29,904 | 30,172 | 29,490 | 30,598 |
| 6 | 30,544 | 30,818 | 30,593 | 30,746 |
| 7 | 30,549 | 30,031 | 29,959 | 30,736 |
| 8 | 30,213 | 29,707 | 28,809 | 29,722 |

### TABLE A.1
Background characteristics of preschool students across all years of analyses

| Year | Age Group | N | White | African American | Latino | Other Race | Special Education | Percent from High-Poverty Neighborhood |
|---|---|---|---|---|---|---|---|---|
| 2008-09 | 3-year-olds | 8,386 | 12% | 48% | 37% | 4% | 8% | 20% |
| | 4-year-olds | 15,713 | 11% | 36% | 49% | 4% | 7% | 15% |
| | All | 24,099 | 11% | 40% | 45% | 4% | 7% | 17% |
| 2009-10 | 3-year-olds | 8,816 | 12% | 48% | 37% | 3% | 9% | 21% |
| | 4-year-olds | 16,506 | 12% | 36% | 48% | 4% | 7% | 16% |
| | All | 25,322 | 12% | 40% | 44% | 4% | 8% | 17% |
| 2010-11 | 3-year-olds | 8,881 | 12% | 44% | 40% | 5% | 9% | 19% |
| | 4-year-olds | 15,571 | 11% | 35% | 50% | 5% | 8% | 15% |
| | All | 24,452 | 11% | 38% | 46% | 5% | 9% | 17% |
| 2011-12 | 3-year-olds | 8,830 | 11% | 45% | 39% | 6% | 9% | 21% |
| | 4-year-olds | 16,118 | 11% | 35% | 49% | 5% | 8% | 15% |
| | All | 24,948 | 11% | 38% | 45% | 6% | 8% | 17% |

# Relationships between Attendance and Student Outcomes

## Preschool Learning Outcomes (KRT)

In 2010-11, OECE at CPS conducted a study of preschool students—the Preschool Longitudinal Study (PLS)—for which they collected detailed data on student achievement and classroom practices. They used a stratified, random sampling scheme to select classrooms to participate in the study; this process ensured that their sample of classrooms was representative of the district's preschool programs.[44] Within these classrooms, they conducted classroom observations and one-on-one child assessments with a sub-sample of children. We used the following assessment data from this sample:

- **Woodcock-Johnson III Tests of Achievement (WJ)** The WJ is a norm-referenced assessment of academic achievement that has been widely used for decades.[45] Four-year-olds who were part of the PLS sample were administered several subtests of the Woodcock-Johnson III in both the fall and spring of preschool. We used students' fall Letter-Word Identification scores as a control for incoming achievement when we analyzed end-of-year kindergarten readiness scores. In **Appendix C**, we show students' growth from the beginning to the end of the year on their WJ Brief Achievement Scores, a cluster score derived from three subtests: Applied Problems, Letter-Word Identification, and Spelling.

- **Kindergarten Readiness Tool (KRT)** In spring 2011, four-year-old students were administered a one-on-one assessment of their kindergarten readiness skills. The Kindergarten Readiness Tool (KRT) was designed by CPS in 2009 and has been revised over the years. The version used in spring 2011 was analyzed by CCSR to ensure internal reliability of the tool (**see Appendix B**). We use this assessment as a measure of students' skills in math, letter recognition, pre-literacy, and social-emotional development at the end of preschool.

Our analysis of preschool learning outcomes was based on CPS's sample of 1,265 students in their PLS study who were four years old in 2010-11. Background characteristics are shown in **Table A.3**; these statistics are presented by six categories of absences and they are also shown for the sample as a whole. For comparison, the bottom row of each table also provides descriptive statistics for the full population of four-year-olds from which the sample was drawn. The sample used in the analysis of preschool learning outcomes is somewhat similar to the full population of four-year-olds in 2010-11, with a few exceptions: there were considerably

**TABLE A.3**

Descriptive statistics on the sample of students used in the analysis of preschool learning outcomes and on the population of four-year-olds enrolled in 2010-11

| Absence Rates | N | White | African American | Latino | Other | Special Education | Percent from High-Poverty Neighborhood | Incoming WJ Letter-Word Identification Score |
|---|---|---|---|---|---|---|---|---|
| 0%<3.3% | 275 | 17% | 24% | 53% | 6% | 6% | 10% | 343.9 |
| 3.3%<6.6% | 344 | 25% | 26% | 43% | 6% | 3% | 10% | 341.5 |
| 6.6%<10% | 203 | 15% | 37% | 43% | 5% | 4% | 15% | 339.2 |
| 10%<15% | 206 | 15% | 46% | 35% | 3% | 5% | 22% | 338.8 |
| 15%<20% | 125 | 10% | 58% | 30% | 3% | 7% | 20% | 335.2 |
| 20%+ | 110 | 9% | 70% | 20% | 1% | 7% | 29% | 325.6 |
| TOTAL Sample | 1,265 | 17% | 38% | 42% | 5% | 5% | 16% | 339.2 (25.9)* |
| All Four-Year-Olds | 15,358 | 11% | 35% | 50% | 5% | 9% | 13% | — |

**Note:** * Standard deviation of WJ-LW scores

fewer Latino students and more white students in the sample than in the full population. As a result, fewer students in the sample were chronically absent than in the full population (35 percent compared to 41 percent). The difference in ethnic composition between the sample and the full population may be due to a shortage of Spanish speaking assessors who administered the Woodcock-Johnson III test to this sample at the beginning of the school year.

There are several dissimilarities across students who exhibited different absence rates over the school year. Students who attended most regularly were more likely to be white, less likely to be African American, less likely to be receiving special education services, and less likely to be from a high-poverty neighborhood; they also entered preschool with higher incoming skills than students who were absent from school more often.

We ran several analyses of each of the four KRT subscales. The first analysis examined the bivariate relationship between students' absence categories and their KRT scores, without taking into account students' background characteristics or incoming skills. Because of the differences in students' background characteristics and incoming skills by absence category displayed in **Table A.2 on p.44**, our second model controlled for these differences.

Both models were run using an HLM measurement model in which a student's score on a KRT subtest was adjusted at level 1 for measurement error in the KRT score (obtained through Rasch analysis of the items that comprise that test). Adjusted scores were nested within students at level 2, and students were nested within preschools at level 3. The initial model did not include any control variables. The model for the second analysis is shown below.

A third model examined whether there were interaction effects of initial skill and attendance on predicted outcomes — that is, whether attendance had different relationships with outcomes depending on students' initial skill levels. We included a linear standardized rate (rather than the absence categories included above). The interaction terms were interactions between the linear absence rate and the incoming Woodcock-Johnson III Letter-Word Identification score.

## Second Grade Attendance

We show the trajectory of attendance for students from the time they are four years old through the time they are seven years old. These descriptions include all students who were four years old in 2008-09 for whom we had preschool attendance data; we followed them longitudinally for four years. The final sample size was 15,713 students.

**LEVEL 1 MODEL**

$(\text{KRT Score/Standard Error})_{ijk} = \pi_{1jk}(1/\text{Standard Error}_{ijk}) + e^*_{ijk}$

$e^*_{ijk} \sim N(0,1)$

**LEVEL 2 MODEL**

$\pi_{1jk} = \beta_{10k} + \beta_{11k}(\text{Absence Category 2}_{jk}) + \beta_{12k}(\text{Absence Category 3}_{jk}) + \beta_{13k}(\text{Absence Category 4}_{jk})$
$+ \beta_{14k}(\text{Absence Category 5}_{jk}) + \beta_{15k}(\text{Absence Category 6}_{jk}) + \beta_{16k}(\text{African American}_{jk}) + \beta_{17k}(\text{Latino}_{jk})$
$+ \beta_{18k}(\text{Other Race}_{jk}) + \beta_{19k}(\text{Neighborhood Poverty}_{jk}) + \beta_{110k}(\text{Neighborhood Social Status}_{jk})$
$+ \beta_{111k}(\text{English Language Learner}_{jk}) + \beta_{112k}(\text{Special Education}_{jk}) + \beta_{113k}(\text{Male}_{jk}) + \beta_{114k}(\text{First Preschool Year}_{jk})$
$+ \beta_{115k}(\text{Fall WJ Letter-Word Identification Score}_{jk}) + r_{1jk}$

**LEVEL 3 MODEL**

$\beta_{10k} = \gamma_{100} + u_{10k}$

$\beta_{11k} = \gamma_{110}$

...

$\beta_{115k} = \gamma_{1150}$

## Second Grade Learning Outcomes (DIBELS)

The outcome measure for second grade learning outcomes was the *Dynamic Indicators of Basic Early Literacy Skills* (DIBELS 6th Edition), provided by CPS.[46] Some CPS schools, but not all, administer the DIBELS to their second-grade students in the spring of each year; the decision of whether or not to use the DIBELS has been left up to network areas and schools. As of 2011-12, charter schools either did not administer the DIBELS in their schools or did not report those scores to CPS.

Our analysis of learning outcomes in second grade was based on a sample of 7,236 four-year-olds who were enrolled in a CPS preschool during 2008-09, had reached second grade by 2011-12, and took the DIBELS that year. The sample used in the analysis of second grade learning outcomes was very similar to the full population from which it was drawn (see Table A.4). This represents 46 percent of all four-year-old preschool students in 2008-09. The sample was similar in background characteristics to the full four-year-old population, except that the DIBELS-takers were slightly less likely to be African American, perhaps a function of the fact that charter schools did not administer the DIBELS or provide that data to CPS.

We conducted two two-level HLM analyses with students nested within the school they attended when they were in preschool. The first model only included a dummy variable for each year students were chronically absent (i.e., preschool, kindergarten, first grade, and second grade). We tested whether there were significant interactions between multiple years of chronic absenteeism, but none existed; therefore, the relationship between having more years of chronic absenteeism and DIBELS scores was additive. The results of this model are shown in **Figure 10 in Chapter 2**. The second model, shown below, added background characteristics (i.e., race, neighborhood poverty, neighborhood social status, special education status, and gender). Because there were no data available, we did not control for any prior achievement. The results of this model are presented in **Endnote 25**.

### TABLE A.4

Background characteristics of students who took the DIBELS at the end of second grade in 2011-12, compared with the full four-year-old population in 2008-09

|  | N | White | African American | Latino | Other Race | Special Education (Second Grade) | Percent from High-Poverty Neighborhood | Preschool Absence Rate |
|---|---|---|---|---|---|---|---|---|
| Full population of 4-year-olds in 2008-09 | 15,636 | 10.5% | 36.3% | 49.0% | 4.1% | 4.9% | 14.7% | 11.4% |
| Population of 4-year-olds in 2008-09 who took DIBELS in 2011-12 | 7,236 | 11.6% | 32.9% | 50.4% | 5.1% | 4.8% | 13.6% | 10.3% |

### LEVEL 1 MODEL

DIBELS Score$_{ij}$ = $\beta_{0j}$ + $\beta_{1j}$(Chronically Absent in PreK$_{ij}$) + $\beta_{2j}$(Chronically Absent in Kindergarten$_{ij}$)
+ $\beta_{3j}$(Chronically Absent in First Grade$_{ij}$) + $\beta_{4j}$(Chronically Absent in Second Grade$_{ij}$) + $\beta_{5j}$(African American$_{ij}$)
+ $\beta_{6j}$(Latino$_{ij}$) + $\beta_{7j}$(Other Race$_{ij}$) + $\beta_{8j}$(Neighborhood Poverty$_{ij}$) + $\beta_{9j}$(Neighborhood Social Status$_{ij}$)
+ $\beta_{10j}$(Special Education$_{ij}$) + $\beta_{11j}$(Male$_{ij}$) + $r_{ij}$

### LEVEL 2 MODEL

$\beta_{0j} = \gamma_{00} + u_{0j}$
$\beta_{1j} = \gamma_{10}$
...
$\beta_{11j} = \gamma_{110}$

# Understanding Reasons for Absences, Explaining the Racial Gap, and Exploring School-Level Culture

## Understanding Reasons for Absences

With the help and support of OECE, CCSR conducted several types of new data collection during the 2011-12 school year to better understand reasons behind preschool absences. These included attendance logs, parent surveys, and parent interviews.

**Attendance Logs.** In a sample of classrooms (described below), teachers were asked to keep logs of the reasons why students were absent. Logs were filled out for a three-week period at three different points of the year (November, February, and April/May). For each round of data collection, teachers received pre-populated rosters of students either in their AM or in their PM session (our target class). The teachers recorded who was absent on each day of the three-week period. They then chose a reason for the absence from a list already provided to them. The options were: doctor's visit (but not sick); sick (non-chronic); chronic illness; lack of transportation; caregiver arrangements; school phobia/separation anxiety; personal time/vacation; lack of sleep; family-related reason; violence/safety; weather; religion; other; do not know. There was also space for the teacher to write notes if s/he could elaborate on the reason.

Attendance logs were collected in 57 preschool classrooms. These classrooms were chosen as a representative sample of classrooms from OECE's Preschool Longitudinal Study sample. Across the three attendance log time points, we had data for a total of 1,229 students. This sample is representative of the full CPS preschool population (**see Table A.5 on p.49** for the background characteristics and overall absence rate of this sample).

**Parent Surveys.** On report card pick-up day in April 2012, OECE and CCSR staff conducted surveys from parents who agreed to participate. Staff approached all parents of children in a target session (morning or afternoon), and asked them if they would be willing to fill out a short survey. In return, they received a $5 gift card. Parent surveys were collected in 55 of our 57 sample classrooms. We have responses from parents of 56 percent of all students in these classes, and over 90 percent of the parents who were present for parent-teacher meetings on the day of report card pick-ups. Our total number of survey responses was 627. On the survey consent form, we asked parents for permission to link their responses to information about their child (background characteristics and attendance data). Of the 627 respondents, 525 provided consent and information about their child so we could merge the data about their child with the survey responses. This sample of students (whose parents gave permission to link the survey data to background information) has a lower average absence rate compared to all CPS preschool children, indicating that our data collection procedure may have attracted a somewhat biased sample of parents for the survey (**see Table A.5**). Therefore, we do not use this sample to estimate the absence rates or frequency of reasons for absence across the population of students; we use the log data for this purpose. Instead, we use the parent surveys to examine the relationships between family circumstances and attitudes and absence rates for subgroups of students.

**Parent Interviews.** On the parent survey, we asked parents to indicate if they would be willing to participate in a follow-up interview about their answers to survey questions. Roughly 65 percent of survey parents agreed to be contacted for a follow-up interview (n=408), providing a large group from which to sample. We used a two-step process to select our interview sample. First, we selected 11 classrooms using a stratified, random sampling design and oversampled classrooms with high average absences. In each of the 11 selected classrooms, we aimed to select a sample of parents that represented different levels of student absenteeism, with an over-sampling of students with high rates of absenteeism. We over-sampled families whose students had high rates of absenteeism so that we could learn about the factors that interfered with coming to school. Students in each classroom were divided into attendance terciles (based on attendance data as of the beginning of April 2012). We then randomly selected two students from the high tercile of absence rates and one student from each of the low and middle terciles. Our final sample consisted of 40 parents—four of whom were interviewed in Spanish. **Table A.5** shows that our

**TABLE A.5**

Background characteristics and average absence rates of log, survey, and interview samples

| Sample | N | White | African American | Latino | Other Race | Special Education | Percent from High-Poverty Neighborhood | Average Absence Rate |
|---|---|---|---|---|---|---|---|---|
| Logs | 1229 | 13% | 40% | 41% | 4% | 8% | 15% | 10.7% |
| Parent Surveys with Permission to Link to Student Data | 525 | 15% | 38% | 42% | 5% | 6% | 14% | 8.5% |
| Parent Interviews | 40 | 16% | 62% | 19% | 3% | 15% | 41% | 11.3% |

interview sample over-represents African American, high-poverty, and special education students.

We conducted follow-up phone interviews with our sample of parents. The interviews asked how parents felt about their child's preschool education and what types of reasons cause their child to miss preschool. Interviews were conducted over the phone and lasted between 20 and 30 minutes. Parents were thanked with a $25 gift card.

## Explaining the Racial Gap

The analysis examining factors associated with higher absence rates of African American preschool students compared to white students is based on a sample of 487 students for whom a parent or guardian completed a parent survey (the remaining surveys had been completed by another relative or caregiver). This analysis uses a two-level hierarchical Poisson regression to model to the number of days students were absent, taking into account the total number of days enrolled as a function of student characteristics (i.e., race, age, and health) and parent characteristics (i.e., marital status, employment status, education level, health, source of primary medical care, and mode of transportation to school) at level 1 (**see Model below**). Students were nested within the preschool in which they were enrolled at level 2.

After running the model, we used the student-level residual file to draw a random sample of white students that was the same size as the population of African American students in our analysis (depending on which comparison we were making). We then assigned this sample of white students the same characteristics as African American students (defined by the predictors in the model referenced above). Finally, we ran a series of simulations in which we estimated what the rate of chronic absenteeism would be if they had the same characteristics as African American students.

**LEVEL 1 MODEL**

$\text{Log [Absence Rate}_{ij}] = \beta_{0j} + \beta_{1j}(\text{African American})_{ij} + \beta_{2j}(\text{Latino})_{ij} + \beta_{3j}(\text{Other Race})_{ij} + \beta_{4j}(\text{Three Year Old})_{ij}$
$+ \beta_{5j}(\text{Single Parent})_{ij} + \beta_{6j}(\text{Parent is Employed with College Degree})_{ij} + \beta_{7j}(\text{Parent has Chronic Illness})_{ij}$
$+ \beta_{8j}(\text{Child has a Chronic Illness})_{ij} + \beta_{9j}(\text{Primary Medical Care: Emergency Room})_{ij}$
$+ \beta1_{0j}(\text{Use Public Transportation to/from School})_{ij} + e_{ij}$

**LEVEL 2 MODEL**

$\beta_{0j} = \gamma_{00} + u_{0j}$
$\beta_{1j} = \gamma_{10}$
...
$\beta_{10} = \gamma_{10}$

## Examining the Relationship between Attendance and School Climate and Classroom Instructional Quality

### School Climate Measures

The University of Chicago Urban Education Institute (UChicago UEI) administers an annual survey to all teachers across the CPS district, called the My Voice, My School survey. To characterize climate in elementary schools, we used teacher responses to the survey administered in the spring of 2012. The teacher response rate on this survey was 64 percent for elementary school teachers (preschool through eighth grade), for a total of 9,531 respondents. For questions asked only of preschool teachers, there were 657 respondents.

Some items on the survey, such as teacher-parent trust, have been included in the survey for many years. Others were added in 2012 specifically for preschool teachers. **Table A.6 on p.51** displays items used in our analyses and whether the items were administered to all teachers in the school or only to preschool teachers.

Using Rasch model of analysis,[47] UChicago CCSR produces measures from multiple items on the CCSR teacher survey. These are more comprehensive and reliable than individual items. The Rasch approach permits the creation of latent variables (e.g., Teacher-Parent Trust, Preschool Inclusion in Elementary School) that are conceptually and empirically cohesive. Using items that relate to the same characteristic, scales are constructed reflecting the relative *"difficulty"* (the likelihood that respondents will agree with a given item) of each item.

Our creation of measures is based on the fit statistic, which has an expected value of 1 and is calculated by taking the mean squared deviations between the expected and observed values for that item. Items for which the fit statistic is greater than 1.3 are excluded; these items do not necessarily measure the same underlying construct. The scales are also evaluated based on the person reliability statistic (the ratio of adjusted standard deviation to the root mean square error computed over the persons), which is approximately equivalent to Cronbach's alpha. We also obtain measures of school-level reliability from an HLM analysis that gauges the degree to which responses are consistent among teachers in the same school.

The Rasch measures are created on a logit scale. Teachers were scored on these measures based on their responses to the 2012 survey. **Table A.6** displays the measures used in our analyses for this report and items that are included in the measure. **Table A.7** lists the reliabilities for each of our measures. Teacher responses on each measure were then aggregated to the school level to create a school-wide indicator of each measure.

### TABLE A.7
**Teacher Survey Measure Reliabilities**

| Measure | Individual Reliability | School-level Reliability |
|---|---|---|
| Teacher Safety | 0.86 | 0.90 |
| Collective Responsibility | 0.91 | 0.69 |
| School Commitment | 0.80 | 0.77 |
| Teacher Influence | 0.82 | 0.80 |
| Outreach to Parents | 0.84 | 0.71 |
| Teacher-Parent Trust | 0.77 | 0.75 |
| Parent Involvement | 0.87 | 0.73 |
| Preschool Inclusion | 0.53* | |

**Note:** *This reliability is lower than we normally accept to create a measure. However, having a continuous measure of teachers' perspectives on the inclusiveness of preschool in their elementary school (rather than two responses to two items) allows us to conduct our analyses described below.

### Classroom Quality Measure

As part of CPS's PLS data collection, CPS conducts annual classroom observations in their sampled classrooms using the Classroom Assessment Scoring System-PreK (CLASS).[48] In 2010-11, CPS only observed classrooms using items in the Instructional Support domain, which assesses the quality of classroom interactions around cognitive development, language modeling, and quality of feedback. We have observation scores on 297 number of classrooms in 2010-2011.

### Analyses

To explore whether school climate is related to preschool students' attendance, we first ran a two level HLM in which students were nested in their preschools. We modeled four-year-old students' absence rates (transformed into logits) as a function of their background characteristics (i.e., race, gender, ELL status, neighborhood poverty status, neighborhood socioeconomic status,

**TABLE A.6**

The items that comprise survey measures included in present analyses

| | | |
|---|---|---|
| Teacher Safety | To what extent is each of the following a problem at your school<br>• Physical conflicts among students<br>• Robbery or theft<br>• Gang activity<br>• Disorder in classrooms<br>• Disorder in hallways<br>• Student disrespect of teachers<br>• Threats of violence towards teachers<br>*Not at all, A little, Some, To a great extent* | All Teachers |
| Collective Responsibility | How many teachers in this school:<br>• Help maintain discipline in the entire school, not just their classroom.<br>• Take responsibility for improving the school.<br>• Feel responsible to help each other do their best.<br>• Feel responsible that all students learn.<br>• Feel responsible for helping students develop self-control.<br>• Feel responsible when students in this school fail.<br>*None, Some, About half, Most* | All Teachers |
| School Commitment | Please mark the extent to which you disagree or agree with each of the following:<br>• I usually look forward to each working day at this school.<br>• I wouldn't want to work in any other school.<br>• I feel loyal to this school.<br>• I would recommend this school to parents seeking a place for their child.<br>*Strongly disagree, Disagree, Agree, Strongly agree* | All Teachers |
| Teacher-Parent Trust | For the students you teach this year, how many of their parents:<br>• Support your teaching efforts<br>• Do their best to help their children learn<br>*None, Some, About half, Most, All* | All Teachers |
| | How many teachers at this school feel good about parent's support for their work?<br>*None, Some, About half, Most, Nearly all* | |
| | Please mark the extent to which you disagree or agree with each of the following statements about your school:<br>• Teachers and parents think of each other as partners in educating children.<br>• Staff at this school work hard to build trusting relationships with parents.<br>*Strongly disagree, Disagree, Agree, Strongly agree* | |
| | To what extent do you feel respected by the parents of your students?<br>*Not at all, A little, Some, To a great extent* | |
| Parent Involvement in School | For the students you teach this year, how many of their parents:<br>• Attended parent-teacher conferences when you requested them.<br>• Volunteered time to support the school (e.g., volunteer in classrooms, help with school-wide events, etc.)<br>• Contacted me about their child's performance.<br>• Picked up their child's last report card.<br>*None, Some, About half, Most* | All Teachers |
| Preschool Inclusion | How much does your preschool program feel like a part of your larger elementary school?<br>*Not at all, A little, Somewhat, Very much* | Preschool Teachers |
| | How much do you agree or disagree with the following statement?<br>My school supports collaboration between preschool and kindergarten teachers to align learning goals for children across the years.<br>*Strongly disagree, Disagree, Agree, Strongly agree* | |

special education status, and distance traveled from home to school). The school-level residuals from this analysis provide a measure of how much better or worse than expected a preschool's absence rate is given the population it serves. A school's residual, when combined with the overall mean absence rate across all preschools, can be thought of as an adjusted absence rate for that preschool in which the effects of students' background characteristics have been removed. We then examined the correlations of these school-level residuals with the measures of school climate described in **Table A.6** to determine which measures were most strongly related to the adjusted school-level attendance rate.

To examine the relationship between classroom instructional quality and preschool attendance we used a strategy similar to the one described above, except that students were nested in classrooms instead of schools. We modeled four-year-old students' absence rates as a function of the same background characteristics described above. Classroom level residuals were combined with the overall mean absence rate across all classrooms to create an adjusted classroom absence rate. This adjusted rate was then correlated with the CLASS score measuring instructional quality for that classroom.

# Appendix B
Development of the Kindergarten Readiness Tool Rasch Subscales

The Kindergarten Readiness Tool (KRT) was developed by the Office of Early Childhood at Chicago Public Schools as a diagnostic tool. The main purpose was to determine the overall effectiveness of pre-school programs, but data has also been made available to kindergarten teachers to provide information about students' incoming skill levels.

The KRT is made up of 86 items that are administered to children one-on-one. These include 54 items assessing students' literacy skills and 32 math items. There are an additional eight items that assess the student's emotional and behavioral development, through teacher report. The math and literacy items are dichotomous response items (scored *"correct"* or *"incorrect"*).

## Subscale Development

The three areas suggest forming at least three subscales. We tested this idea by applying Rasch analysis to the items from each of the areas, and we found that the appropriate number of subscales was four.

## Identification of Two Reading Subscales

It was clear from the beginning that the literacy items were behaving in a conceptually diverse manner. Principal components analysis of the responses confirmed that there were two separate subscales within the literacy items.

The first set of items, with factor loadings less than or equal to zero, included items that assessed the recognition of letter names and sounds (*"letter recognition"*). The second set of items, with the loadings greater than zero, test slightly more advanced skills (e.g., writing, comprehension, print awareness, phonological awareness, and vocabulary), which we call *"pre-literacy."*

The letter recognition subscale consists of the 30 items, with a separation of 3.10, corresponding to a reliability of 0.91. The pre-literacy has a separation of 2.08 and a reliability of 0.81.

## Math Subscale

There are 32 math items in the KRT. Analyzing them gives a separation of 2.12 and a reliability of 0.82. However, one item was a misfit. The item is a very difficult item, with a difficulty of 3.25—only about 25 percent of the students got it correct. The difficulty is more than one standard deviation above the mean person measure. Removing that item reduces the separation and reliability to 2.02 and 0.80, respectively, but makes for a more satisfying scale.

## Social-Emotional Development Subscale

For this subscale, the teacher responded to eight items about the student's behavior in the classroom and work habits. Each of the items is scored on its own 4-point scale, with language specific to the item stem. These eight items give a separation and reliability of 2.05 and 0.81, respectively.

## Correlations of All Four Measures

We would expect that students would score similarly on all four subscales, and, to a certain extent, this is true. The following table shows the inter-correlations among measures for all subscales.

**TABLE B.1**

**Correlations between KRT Subscales**

| | Letter Recognition | Pre-Literacy | Math |
|---|---|---|---|
| Pre-Literacy | 0.59 | | |
| Math | 0.69 | 0.72 | |
| Social-Emotional Development | 0.42 | 0.49 | 0.52 |

# Appendix C
## Relationship between Preschool Attendance and Growth on Woodcock-Johnson III

In Chapter 2, we describe how attendance is related to learning outcomes on the Kindergarten Readiness Tool (KRT) administered at the end of preschool. We chose this instrument because it measures multiple domains deemed necessary for kindergarten readiness, including both academic and social-emotional domains. In our final models, described in **Appendix A**, we used a measure from the Woodcock-Johnson III to control for incoming skills. Because children were not given the KRT at the beginning of the year, we were not able to directly measure growth on those subscales. Children were, however, given the Woodcock-Johnson III assessment in both the fall and spring of their preschool year. Here, we show an additional set of analyses examining growth on the Woodcock-Johnson III during the preschool year; these analyses corroborate our findings from the KRT analysis.

### Sample and Analyses
The sample of students included in this analysis is very similar to the one used in our KRT analyses. We include any four-year-old for whom we have fall and spring WJ-Brief Achieve scores in 2010-11. Our total sample included 1,116 students.

CPS administered a range of assessments to this sample of children at both the beginning and end of the preschool year, including five subtests of the Woodcock-Johnson III, a normed test of achievement.[49] They were: Letter-Word Identification (LW), Story Recall, Understanding Directions, Spelling, and Applied Problems (AP). The WJ-III scoring software produces also cluster scores out of these subtests: Brief Achievement (a cluster of LW, AP, and Spelling) and Oral Language (a cluster of Story Recall and Understanding Directions). The scores provided to CCSR were W scores, which are Rasch-based scores that allow for a direct linear comparison over time.[50] For our analyses, we focused on the Brief Achievement cluster score, which captures both early literacy and early math concepts. These are most aligned with three of the KRT subscales that focus on academic learning (letter recognition, early literacy, and math).

We used a two level HLM to analyze growth from fall to spring on the Brief Achieve score, controlling for the same set of background characteristics used in the KRT analyses (gender, race/ethnicity, ELL status, special education status, prior preschool experience in CPS, and neighborhood poverty/social status). We also added two extra controls into these models for children's age at the first testing time point, and for the lapse in time between the fall and spring administration of the WJ III.

### Analyses of Growth on the Woodcock-Johnson Brief Achievement Scores Corroborate Findings from KRT Analyses

Similar to our KRT findings, children who missed more school had lower scores in the spring implementation of the Woodcock-Johnson, even when we compare students with similar scores in the fall. Children with high absence rates had smaller gains from fall to spring than children who regularly came to school. **Figure C.1** shows spring WJ scores for students by their absence category. These show the predicted spring scores, adjusting for fall scores and background characteristics. As presented in Chapter 2, outcomes are lower for children who attend school less.

We also examined whether the relationship between absence rates and spring scores was different depending on students' incoming skill level. We found that the relationship was stronger for students who entered preschool with lower levels of incoming skills, which is consistent with findings from the KRT analyses. Among students with low levels of incoming skills (yellow lines in **Figure C.2**), test score gains were considerably higher for students who had the best attendance (missing less than 3.3 percent of school) than for students who had the worst attendance (missing 10 percent or more of

**FIGURE C.1**

Students who miss more school learn less over the school year, resulting in lower scores in the spring than students who attend school regularly.

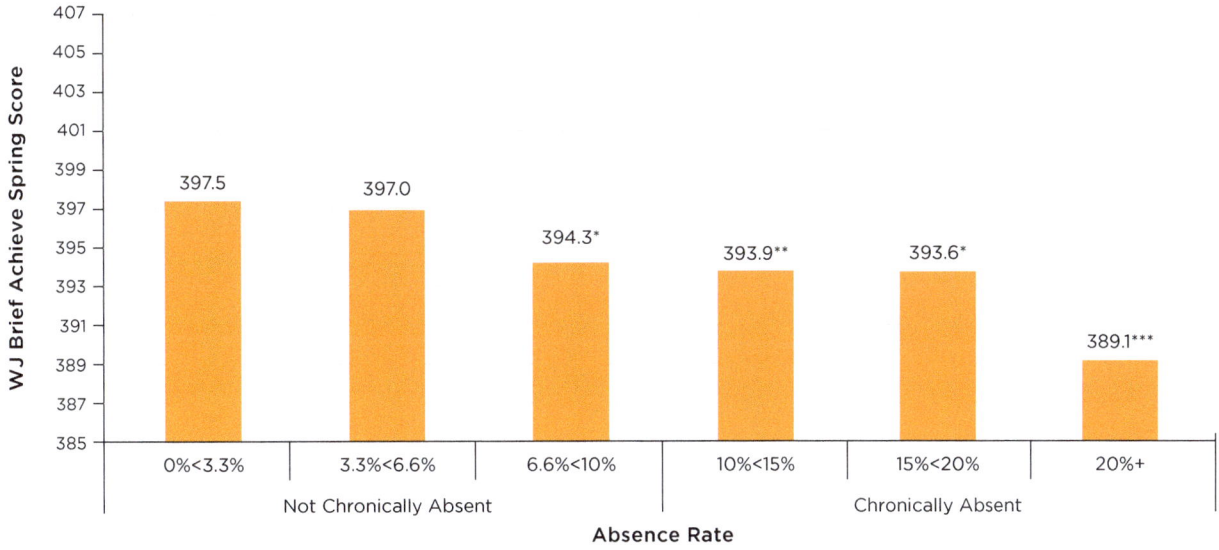

**Note:** These results take into account students' race/ethnicity, gender, ELL status, special education status, whether they attended CPS preschool the prior year, neighborhood poverty leve, and fall Woodcock Johnson scoresl; n=1,060. *Indicates that scores are significantly different from scores of students with absences between 0 and 3.3 percent at p<.05 level; **p<.01; ***p<.001.

**FIGURE C.2**

**The largest gains are attained by students who enter with the lowest skills and attend school the most.**

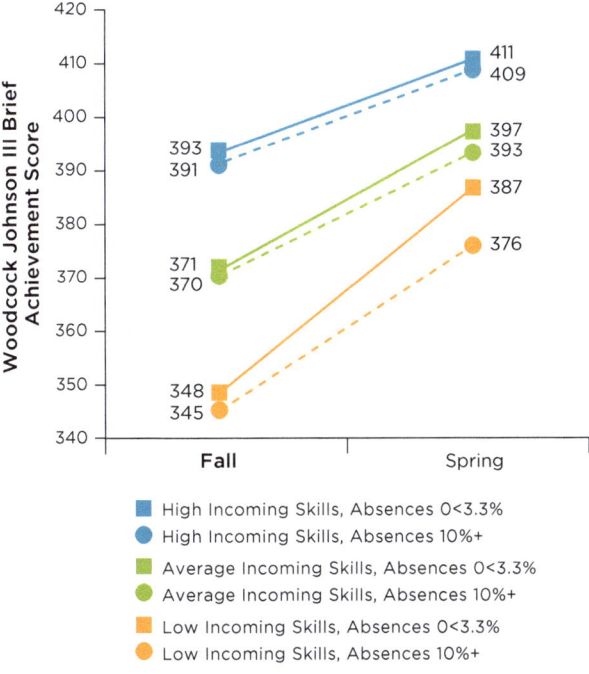

**Note:** This graph shows average growth for students based on their incoming skill level and their attendance during the preschool year. Solid lines represent students within each achievement group who had the best attendance (missing less than 3.3 percent of school) and dashed lines represent students within each achievement group who were chronically absent (missing 10 percent or more of school); n=1,060.

school). Among students who entered preschool with the highest level of incoming skills (green and blue lines in **Figure C.2**), test scores gains were similar for students with the best and worst attendance. Overall, students who enter school with the lowest scores do learn more than students who enter with the highest scores, thereby narrowing the achievement gap. However, the gap narrows less among children who miss a substantial amount of preschool. Preschool is intended to better prepare children—especially low-skilled, high-risk children—for kindergarten and beyond. We see here that this can only be realized if children with low skills are not only enrolled in preschool but also are attending school regularly.

Appendix C

# Endnotes

### Executive Summary

1. Allensworth and Easton (2007); Neild, Balfanz, and Herzog (2007).
2. Romero and Lee (2007); Ready (2010).

### Introduction

3. For example, see Campbell et al. (2001); Heckman (2011); Ramey and Ramey (1998); Reynolds et al. (2007); Schweinhart et al. (2005).
4. Middle and high school students: Allensworth and Easton (2007); Neild, Balfanz, and Herzog (2007); elementary students: Plank et al. (2008); kindergarten students: Chang and Romero (2008); Ready (2010).
5. Romero and Lee (2007).
6. Connolly and Olson (2012).
7. See Bitler, Hoynes, and Domina (2013).
8. For example, see Balfanz and Byrnes (2012).
9. Bloom, Cohen, and Freeman (2012).
10. Case, Lubotsky, and Paxson (2002).
11. Bloom, Dey, and Freeman (2006).
12. Bryk et al. (2010).
13. For all analyses, we limit our sample to students who were enrolled for more than 20 days over the school year. Students enrolled for 20 days or fewer have higher absence rates than other students, likely because the denominator in the calculation of their absence rate is so low.
14. In 2012-13, the City of Chicago underwent a rebid for publicly funded preschool programs. Each community-based organization and school offering a preschool program had to apply (or reapply) for slots, and programs were chosen based on the quality of their applications as well as need in their neighborhood. In future years, classrooms may blend funding streams, thereby eliminating some of the structural program differences seen in the years included in this report.
15. Fifty-seven percent of CPS kindergarten children in 2011-12 had been enrolled in a CPS school-based preschool program the prior year. The remaining 43 percent were either served by other preschool programs or did not have any formal education prior to entering CPS in kindergarten. Nearly all (85 percent) preschool students who enrolled in a CPS school-based program in 2011-12 were still enrolled in a CPS school the next year. This included three-year-olds who remained in CPS for their four-year-old preschool year and four-year-olds who transitioned to a CPS kindergarten program.

### Chapter 1

16. Recall that we exclude students who are in self-contained special education programs. Therefore, this comparison only includes special education students in general education classes.

### Chapter 2

17. In math and letter recognition, the difference in scores between students with the best attendance and students with the worst attendance is 1.1 standard deviations. For pre-literacy and social-emotional, differences in scores between the best and worst attenders are 0.89 standard deviations and 0.85 standard deviations, respectively.
18. Students who missed 10 percent or more of school entered with Woodcock-Johnson III Letter-Word Identification scores that were 0.17 standard deviations behind those of students who attended school most regularly; students who missed at least 20 percent of school entered with scores 0.61 standard deviations behind their regularly attending peers.
19. We recognize that there may well be characteristics of children and families not captured in our analyses that could be correlated with both student absence rate and students' learning over the school year. Indeed, in Chapter 4 we describe aspects of students' families that are related to school attendance; these family characteristics may also impact student learning. However, establishing the strong relationship between attendance and learning outcomes in preschool is the first step in better understanding the direct role that attendance may have on learning.
20. We also tested to see whether the relationship between attendance and outcomes was different across racial/ethnic groups and for students from lower- or higher-poverty neighborhoods, but we found no differences.
21. To test for interactions, we used the continuous absence rate, rather than the six absence categories used in prior models. Woodcock-Johnson III Letter-Word Identification (WJ-LW) scores in Fall 2010 were used to measure incoming skills.
22. Rush (1999).

23 When looking at students who were enrolled in CPS in both preschool (2008-09) and kindergarten (2009-10), 42.6 percent of chronically absent kindergarteners had missed 20 percent or more of school during preschool, and another 35 percent had missed between 10 and 19.9 percent during preschool.

24 Our HLM models, described in Appendix A, have a predictor for being chronically absent in each year between 2008-09 and 2011-12. We tested for whether there were interactions between multiple years of chronic absenteeism and DIBELS ORF outcomes, but none were significant. Therefore, it seems that there is an additive relationship between chronic absenteeism in the early years and our outcome measure.

25 Figure 10 does not control for student background characteristics; however, even when we take into account background characteristics (e.g., race/ethnicity, gender, special education status, and neighborhood poverty and social status), students who have multiple years of chronic absenteeism still need some intervention to be reading on grade level by third grade, on average. The means for each group in the model controlling for background characteristics are: Not chronically absent (CA): 99.0; CA in preschool: 95.8; CA in preschool and kindergarten: 90.7; CA in preschool, kindergarten, and first grade: 83.8; CA in preschool, kindergarten, first grade, and second grade: 76.3.

26 In the DIBELS 6th Edition Assessment and Scoring Guide (Good and Kaminksi, 2002), these are labeled as *"Some risk,"* indicating the need for additional intervention, and *"At risk,"* indicating the need for substantial interventions.

27 Annie E. Casey Foundation (2010).

28 This is based on a cohort of 2008-09 four-year-olds who were in the CPS system through second grade in 2011-12 and who had a DIBELS score.

## Chapter 3

29 All names of students, parents, and schools in this report are pseudonyms.

30 We report out days missed due to illness based on our attendance logs. It may be that parents have different decision rules about when to keep their child home from school when they are sick. Therefore, when we say that some students are "sick more often," we mean that they were reported as being sick more often when they missed school. However, we have some reason to believe that some groups of students are in fact more likely to get sick more often. For instance, African American children were more likely to have a chronic illness or to have health that was rated poor/fair by their parents.

31 We found a similar relationship between parent attitudes about preschool and children's attendance based on survey responses. Most parents responded that regular attendance in preschool is very important, and their children had an absence rate of 8.2 percent. Children whose parents said attendance is important had an absence rate of 9.4 percent. Children whose parents said attendance is only somewhat important had an absence rate of 15.4 percent. Note that none of these relationships can be interpreted as causal.

32 UChicago CCSR climate surveys measure responses from all teachers within the elementary school (preschool through eighth grade). Note that the survey measures explored here are highly correlated with each other.

33 This particular question was asked only of preschool teachers.

34 Pianta, LaParo, and Hamre (2007).

35 To avoid confounding a school's, or a classroom's, attendance rates with the background characteristics of the students enrolled there, we created an adjusted average attendance rate for each school and each classroom. These adjusted rates take into account the background characteristics of students who attend that school and allow us to compare attendance rates across schools and classrooms as if they served the same population of students. See Appendix A for additional details.

## Chapter 4

36 Kearney and Graczyk (2013).

37 Some programs flag children after they miss a consecutive number of days. Our research suggests that total number of days, even if not missed consecutively, is the more common way that students accumulate absences.

38 Chang and Romero (2008); see also www.attendanceworks.org/tools/ for tools on how to calculate and monitor attendance.

39 U.S. Department of Health and Human Services, Office of Head Start (2011), pg. 5.

40 For example, see Burchinal et al. (2002).

41 Sheldon and Epstein (2004); Sheldon (2007).

42 Recent research shows that intentional work teaching urban, low-income families how to manage their child's asthma leads to significant reductions in hospitalizations for children with asthma (Woods et al., 2012).

43 Barnett et al. (2011).

## Appendices

44 The PLS sample was stratified based on students' race, free lunch status, gender, and preschool program type.

45 Woodcock, McGrew, and Mather (2001).

46 Good and Kaminski (2002).

47 Wright and Master (1982).

48 Pianta, LaParo, and Hamre (2007).

49 Woodcock, McGrew, and Mather (2001).

50 Jaffe (2009).

## Notes From Boxes

A Recently changes have been made to the preschool application process in CPS to centralize the process. However, for the years included in this study, parents were required to submit applications to schools of interest.

B To determine this, we found the elementary school that served the census block in which a preschool child lived. Thus, if a child does not move between his preschool and kindergarten school year, this is the neighborhood school option starting in kindergarten.

C The sub-population of kindergarten students who were in a CPS school-based preschool program the prior year looked very similar to the full kindergarten population: 65 percent of students who had been CPS preschoolers the prior year attended their neighborhood schools when they were in kindergarten.

D Thank you to Hedy Chang, who regularly uses this example to explain the difference between average daily attendance and percent chronically absent.

E For example, see Balfanz and Byrnes (2012) and Chang and Romero (2008).

F Chang and Romero (2008); Romero and Lee (2007).

G To determine whether students exhibited different attendance patterns over the school year, we performed a cluster analysis on a sample of 18,755 three- and four-year-olds who were enrolled in CPS preschool programs for at least 141 days during the 2010-11 school year. We chose to restrict the sample based on enrollment because we reasoned that attendance patterns are dependent on the length of enrollment and because early clustering attempts did not produce distinct clusters when using data for all students. This choice eliminated less than 10 percent of students; more than 90 percent of students were enrolled for at least 141 days. Using a two-stage density linkage algorithm, we clustered students based on (1) number of incidences of absence and (2) length of longest absence, and we found a five cluster solution.

H The average absence rate of students between these five clusters was distinct. That is, there did not exist two clusters with similar average absence rates where students in one cluster were absent more frequently or for a greater stretch of time than students in the other cluster. In addition, the clusters showed a high correlation between frequency of absence and length of longest absence, and a close relationship between our cluster variables and average absence rates. Thus, to cluster on number of incidences of absence and length of longest absence does not provide much additional information about attendance patterns beyond a simple rate of absence.

I Contributing to the lack of representativeness is the fact that CPS did not have enough Spanish-speaking assessors to administer Preschool Longitudinal Study assessments to children.

J Woodcock, McGrew, and Mather (2001).

K Good et al. (2002).

L Chicago Public Schools (2012).

## ABOUT THE AUTHORS

**STACY B. EHRLICH** is a Senior Research Analyst at UChicago CCSR. Her current work focuses on the trajectories of young children in Chicago Public Schools (CPS). Previous work at UChicago CCSR includes studying the use of technology in CPS, how Chicago teens interact with digital media, and how predictive ninth-grade indicators are of high school success for English Language Learners. Prior work, at Education Development Center, Inc. (EDC), included conducting research responding to states' educational policy concerns and a study on a preschool science professional development program. Ehrlich earned an MA and PhD in developmental psychology from the University of Chicago and a BS in human development and family studies from the University of Wisconsin-Madison.

**JULIA A. GWYNNE** is a Senior Research Analyst at UChicago CCSR. Her current work focuses on early warning indicators of high school and college readiness and the use of indicators with groups such as English Language Learners and students with disabilities. In addition, she has also conducted research on student mobility, school closings, and classroom instructional environments. She received her doctoral degree in sociology from the University of Chicago.

**AMBER STITZIEL PAREJA** is a Senior Research Analyst at UChicago CCSR. She is currently a project director on two studies. One examines the mechanisms through which school leadership influences instruction and student learning. Her other work focuses on the efficacy of online versus face-to-face courses for algebra credit recovery. Pareja was previously the project director of a study of the transition from eighth to ninth grade. She received her PhD in human development and social policy from Northwestern University, and she formerly worked as a bilingual (Spanish-English) third-grade teacher.

**ELAINE M. ALLENSWORTH** is the Lewis-Sebring Director at UChicago CCSR where she has conducted research on educational policy for the last 15 years. She is best known for her studies of high school graduation and college readiness, and also conducts research in the areas of school leadership and school organization. Her work on early indicators of high school graduation has been adopted for tracking systems used in Chicago and other districts across the country. She is one of the authors of the book Organizing Schools for Improvement: Lessons from Chicago, which provides a detailed analysis of school practices and community conditions that promote school improvement. Dr. Allensworth holds a PhD in Sociology and an MA in Urban Studies from Michigan State University. She was once a high school Spanish and science teacher.

**PAUL MOORE** is a Research Analyst at UChicago CCSR and is in the process of completing an MA in the social sciences at the University of Chicago. His research interests include quantitative modeling and methodology. He is currently working on a study of middle grade predictors of high school readiness, funded by the Bill and Melinda Gates Foundation. Moore is also studying the effects of attending higher performing schools on students' academic performance and noncognitive skills funded by the Institute of Education Sciences. Paul earned a BS in mathematics and education science from Vanderbilt University.

**SANJA JAGESIC** was a Research Assistant at UChicago CCSR. She holds an MA in sociology from the University of Chicago and a BA in sociology and German from Wellesley College. She is currently working toward her PhD in sociology at the University of Chicago.

**ELIZABETH SORICE** was a Research Intern at UChicago CCSR when she contributed to this research study. She holds an MA in Social Work from the University of Chicago and a BA in women's studies from The College of Wooster. She is currently an Academy Manager for Mercy Home for Boys and Girls.

*This report reflects the interpretation of the authors. Although CCSR's Steering Committee provided technical advice, no formal endorsement by these individuals, organizations, or the full Consortium should be assumed.*

# UCHICAGOCCSR

## CONSORTIUM ON CHICAGO SCHOOL RESEARCH

## Directors

**ELAINE M. ALLENSWORTH**
*Lewis-Sebring Director*
Consortium on Chicago
School Research

**JENNY NAGAOKA**
*Deputy Director*
Consortium on Chicago
School Research

**MELISSA RODERICK**
*Senior Director*
Consortium on Chicago
School Research

*Hermon Dunlap Smith
Professor*
School of Social Service
Administration
University of Chicago

**PENNY BENDER SEBRING**
*Founding Director*
Consortium on Chicago
School Research

## Steering Committee

**LILA LEFF**
*Co-Chair*
Umoja Student Development
Corporation

**KATHLEEN ST. LOUIS
CALIENTO**
*Co-Chair*
Spark, Chicago

### Ex-Officio Members
**TIMOTHY KNOWLES**
Urban Education Institute

### Institutional Members
**JOHN R. BARKER**
Chicago Public Schools

**CLARICE BERRY**
Chicago Principals and
Administrators Association

**AARTI DHUPELIA**
Chicago Public Schools

**CHRISTOPHER KOCH**
Illinois State Board of
Education

**KAREN G.J. LEWIS**
Chicago Teachers Union

**SHERRY J. ULERY**
Chicago Public Schools

### Individual Members
**VERONICA ANDERSON**
Communications Consultant

**JOANNA BROWN**
Logan Square
Neighborhood Association

**ANDREW BROY**
Illinois Network of
Charter Schools

**RAQUEL FARMER-HINTON**
University of Wisconsin,
Milwaukee

**REYNA HERNANDEZ**
Illinois State Board of
Education

**CHRIS JONES**
Stephen T. Mather
High School

**DENNIS LACEWELL**
Urban Prep Charter Academy
for Young Men

**RUANDA GARTH
MCCULLOUGH**
Loyola University, Chicago

**LUISIANA MELÉNDEZ**
Erikson Institute

**LISA SCRUGGS**
Duane Morris LLP

**LUIS R. SORIA**
Chicago Public Schools

**BRIAN SPITTLE**
DePaul University

**MATTHEW STAGNER**
Mathematica Policy Research

**AMY TREADWELL**
Chicago New Teacher Center

**ERIN UNANDER**
Al Raby High School

**ARIE J. VAN DER PLOEG**
American Institutes for
Research (Retired)

**KIM ZALENT**
Business and Professional
People for the Public Interest

www.ingramcontent.com/pod-product-compliance
Lightning Source LLC
Chambersburg PA
CBHW060820090426
42738CB00002B/55